C-3382   CAREER EXAMINATION SERIES

This is your
PASSBOOK for...

Assistant Building Inspector

Test Preparation Study Guide
Questions & Answers

COPYRIGHT NOTICE

This book is SOLELY intended for, is sold ONLY to, and its use is RESTRICTED to individual, bona fide applicants or candidates who qualify by virtue of having seriously filed applications for appropriate license, certificate, professional and/or promotional advancement, higher school matriculation, scholarship, or other legitimate requirements of education and/or governmental authorities.

This book is NOT intended for use, class instruction, tutoring, training, duplication, copying, reprinting, excerption, or adaptation, etc., by:

1) Other publishers
2) Proprietors and/or Instructors of "Coaching" and/or Preparatory Courses
3) Personnel and/or Training Divisions of commercial, industrial, and governmental organizations
4) Schools, colleges, or universities and/or their departments and staffs, including teachers and other personnel
5) Testing Agencies or Bureaus
6) Study groups which seek by the purchase of a single volume to copy and/or duplicate and/or adapt this material for use by the group as a whole without having purchased individual volumes for each of the members of the group
7) Et al.

Such persons would be in violation of appropriate Federal and State statutes.

PROVISION OF LICENSING AGREEMENTS – Recognized educational, commercial, industrial, and governmental institutions and organizations, and others legitimately engaged in educational pursuits, including training, testing, and measurement activities, may address request for a licensing agreement to the copyright owners, who will determine whether, and under what conditions, including fees and charges, the materials in this book may be used them. In other words, a licensing facility exists for the legitimate use of the material in this book on other than an individual basis. However, it is asseverated and affirmed here that the material in this book CANNOT be used without the receipt of the express permission of such a licensing agreement from the Publishers. Inquiries re licensing should be addressed to the company, attention rights and permissions department.

All rights reserved, including the right of reproduction in whole or in part, in any form or by any means, electronic or mechanical, including photocopying, recording, or by any information storage and retrieval system, without permission in writing from the Publisher.

Copyright © 2025 by
National Learning Corporation

212 Michael Drive, Syosset, NY 11791
(516) 921-8888 • www.passbooks.com
E-mail: info@passbooks.com

PASSBOOK® SERIES

THE *PASSBOOK® SERIES* has been created to prepare applicants and candidates for the ultimate academic battlefield – the examination room.

At some time in our lives, each and every one of us may be required to take an examination – for validation, matriculation, admission, qualification, registration, certification, or licensure.

Based on the assumption that every applicant or candidate has met the basic formal educational standards, has taken the required number of courses, and read the necessary texts, the *PASSBOOK® SERIES* furnishes the one special preparation which may assure passing with confidence, instead of failing with insecurity. Examination questions – together with answers – are furnished as the basic vehicle for study so that the mysteries of the examination and its compounding difficulties may be eliminated or diminished by a sure method.

This book is meant to help you pass your examination provided that you qualify and are serious in your objective.

The entire field is reviewed through the huge store of content information which is succinctly presented through a provocative and challenging approach – the question-and-answer method.

A climate of success is established by furnishing the correct answers at the end of each test.

You soon learn to recognize types of questions, forms of questions, and patterns of questioning. You may even begin to anticipate expected outcomes.

You perceive that many questions are repeated or adapted so that you can gain acute insights, which may enable you to score many sure points.

You learn how to confront new questions, or types of questions, and to attack them confidently and work out the correct answers.

You note objectives and emphases, and recognize pitfalls and dangers, so that you may make positive educational adjustments.

Moreover, you are kept fully informed in relation to new concepts, methods, practices, and directions in the field.

You discover that you are actually taking the examination all the time: you are preparing for the examination by "taking" an examination, not by reading extraneous and/or supererogatory textbooks.

In short, this PASSBOOK®, used directedly, should be an important factor in helping you to pass your test.

ASSISTANT BUILDING INSPECTOR

DUTIES

Makes field inspections of building construction and materials used; reports violations of building code, zoning and housing ordinances to the Building Inspector; consults with contractors, owners, state inspectors and fire inspectors in enforcing the building code; investigates and reports on complaints received as to possible violations of the building code and related ordinances as directed by the Building Inspector; makes periodic inspections of homes and other buildings to gather information; and related duties.

SCOPE OF THE EXAMINATION

Written test will, cover knowledge, skills, and/or abilities in such areas as:
1. Inspection procedures;
2. Building construction, including methods, materials, and components;
3. Building, housing and zoning laws and codes; and
4. Interpretation of building plans and requirements.

HOW TO TAKE A TEST

I. YOU MUST PASS AN EXAMINATION

A. *WHAT EVERY CANDIDATE SHOULD KNOW*

Examination applicants often ask us for help in preparing for the written test. What can I study in advance? What kinds of questions will be asked? How will the test be given? How will the papers be graded?

As an applicant for a civil service examination, you may be wondering about some of these things. Our purpose here is to suggest effective methods of advance study and to describe civil service examinations.

Your chances for success on this examination can be increased if you know how to prepare. Those "pre-examination jitters" can be reduced if you know what to expect. You can even experience an adventure in good citizenship if you know why civil service exams are given.

B. *WHY ARE CIVIL SERVICE EXAMINATIONS GIVEN?*

Civil service examinations are important to you in two ways. As a citizen, you want public jobs filled by employees who know how to do their work. As a job seeker, you want a fair chance to compete for that job on an equal footing with other candidates. The best-known means of accomplishing this two-fold goal is the competitive examination.

Exams are widely publicized throughout the nation. They may be administered for jobs in federal, state, city, municipal, town or village governments or agencies.

Any citizen may apply, with some limitations, such as the age or residence of applicants. Your experience and education may be reviewed to see whether you meet the requirements for the particular examination. When these requirements exist, they are reasonable and applied consistently to all applicants. Thus, a competitive examination may cause you some uneasiness now, but it is your privilege and safeguard.

C. *HOW ARE CIVIL SERVICE EXAMS DEVELOPED?*

Examinations are carefully written by trained technicians who are specialists in the field known as "psychological measurement," in consultation with recognized authorities in the field of work that the test will cover. These experts recommend the subject matter areas or skills to be tested; only those knowledges or skills important to your success on the job are included. The most reliable books and source materials available are used as references. Together, the experts and technicians judge the difficulty level of the questions.

Test technicians know how to phrase questions so that the problem is clearly stated. Their ethics do not permit "trick" or "catch" questions. Questions may have been tried out on sample groups, or subjected to statistical analysis, to determine their usefulness.

Written tests are often used in combination with performance tests, ratings of training and experience, and oral interviews. All of these measures combine to form the best-known means of finding the right person for the right job.

II. HOW TO PASS THE WRITTEN TEST

A. NATURE OF THE EXAMINATION

To prepare intelligently for civil service examinations, you should know how they differ from school examinations you have taken. In school you were assigned certain definite pages to read or subjects to cover. The examination questions were quite detailed and usually emphasized memory. Civil service exams, on the other hand, try to discover your present ability to perform the duties of a position, plus your potentiality to learn these duties. In other words, a civil service exam attempts to predict how successful you will be. Questions cover such a broad area that they cannot be as minute and detailed as school exam questions.

In the public service similar kinds of work, or positions, are grouped together in one "class." This process is known as *position-classification*. All the positions in a class are paid according to the salary range for that class. One class title covers all of these positions, and they are all tested by the same examination.

B. FOUR BASIC STEPS

1) Study the announcement

How, then, can you know what subjects to study? Our best answer is: "Learn as much as possible about the class of positions for which you've applied." The exam will test the knowledge, skills and abilities needed to do the work.

Your most valuable source of information about the position you want is the official exam announcement. This announcement lists the training and experience qualifications. Check these standards and apply only if you come reasonably close to meeting them.

The brief description of the position in the examination announcement offers some clues to the subjects which will be tested. Think about the job itself. Review the duties in your mind. Can you perform them, or are there some in which you are rusty? Fill in the blank spots in your preparation.

Many jurisdictions preview the written test in the exam announcement by including a section called "Knowledge and Abilities Required," "Scope of the Examination," or some similar heading. Here you will find out specifically what fields will be tested.

2) Review your own background

Once you learn in general what the position is all about, and what you need to know to do the work, ask yourself which subjects you already know fairly well and which need improvement. You may wonder whether to concentrate on improving your strong areas or on building some background in your fields of weakness. When the announcement has specified "some knowledge" or "considerable knowledge," or has used adjectives like "beginning principles of..." or "advanced ... methods," you can get a clue as to the number and difficulty of questions to be asked in any given field. More questions, and hence broader coverage, would be included for those subjects which are more important in the work. Now weigh your strengths and weaknesses against the job requirements and prepare accordingly.

3) Determine the level of the position

Another way to tell how intensively you should prepare is to understand the level of the job for which you are applying. Is it the entering level? In other words, is this the position in which beginners in a field of work are hired? Or is it an intermediate or advanced level? Sometimes this is indicated by such words as "Junior" or "Senior" in the class title. Other jurisdictions use Roman numerals to designate the level – Clerk I, Clerk II, for example. The word "Supervisor" sometimes appears in the title. If the level is not indicated by the title, check the description of duties. Will you be working under very close supervision, or will you have responsibility for independent decisions in this work?

4) Choose appropriate study materials

Now that you know the subjects to be examined and the relative amount of each subject to be covered, you can choose suitable study materials. For beginning level jobs, or even advanced ones, if you have a pronounced weakness in some aspect of your training, read a modern, standard textbook in that field. Be sure it is up to date and has general coverage. Such books are normally available at your library, and the librarian will be glad to help you locate one. For entry-level positions, questions of appropriate difficulty are chosen – neither highly advanced questions, nor those too simple. Such questions require careful thought but not advanced training.

If the position for which you are applying is technical or advanced, you will read more advanced, specialized material. If you are already familiar with the basic principles of your field, elementary textbooks would waste your time. Concentrate on advanced textbooks and technical periodicals. Think through the concepts and review difficult problems in your field.

These are all general sources. You can get more ideas on your own initiative, following these leads. For example, training manuals and publications of the government agency which employs workers in your field can be useful, particularly for technical and professional positions. A letter or visit to the government department involved may result in more specific study suggestions, and certainly will provide you with a more definite idea of the exact nature of the position you are seeking.

III. KINDS OF TESTS

Tests are used for purposes other than measuring knowledge and ability to perform specified duties. For some positions, it is equally important to test ability to make adjustments to new situations or to profit from training. In others, basic mental abilities not dependent on information are essential. Questions which test these things may not appear as pertinent to the duties of the position as those which test for knowledge and information. Yet they are often highly important parts of a fair examination. For very general questions, it is almost impossible to help you direct your study efforts. What we can do is to point out some of the more common of these general abilities needed in public service positions and describe some typical questions.

1) General information

Broad, general information has been found useful for predicting job success in some kinds of work. This is tested in a variety of ways, from vocabulary lists to questions about current events. Basic background in some field of work, such as sociology or economics, may be sampled in a group of questions. Often these are principles which have become familiar to most persons through exposure rather than through formal training. It is difficult to advise you how to study for these questions; being alert to the world around you is our best suggestion.

2) Verbal ability

An example of an ability needed in many positions is verbal or language ability. Verbal ability is, in brief, the ability to use and understand words. Vocabulary and grammar tests are typical measures of this ability. Reading comprehension or paragraph interpretation questions are common in many kinds of civil service tests. You are given a paragraph of written material and asked to find its central meaning.

3) Numerical ability
Number skills can be tested by the familiar arithmetic problem, by checking paired lists of numbers to see which are alike and which are different, or by interpreting charts and graphs. In the latter test, a graph may be printed in the test booklet which you are asked to use as the basis for answering questions.

4) Observation
A popular test for law-enforcement positions is the observation test. A picture is shown to you for several minutes, then taken away. Questions about the picture test your ability to observe both details and larger elements.

5) Following directions
In many positions in the public service, the employee must be able to carry out written instructions dependably and accurately. You may be given a chart with several columns, each column listing a variety of information. The questions require you to carry out directions involving the information given in the chart.

6) Skills and aptitudes
Performance tests effectively measure some manual skills and aptitudes. When the skill is one in which you are trained, such as typing or shorthand, you can practice. These tests are often very much like those given in business school or high school courses. For many of the other skills and aptitudes, however, no short-time preparation can be made. Skills and abilities natural to you or that you have developed throughout your lifetime are being tested.

Many of the general questions just described provide all the data needed to answer the questions and ask you to use your reasoning ability to find the answers. Your best preparation for these tests, as well as for tests of facts and ideas, is to be at your physical and mental best. You, no doubt, have your own methods of getting into an exam-taking mood and keeping "in shape." The next section lists some ideas on this subject.

IV. KINDS OF QUESTIONS

Only rarely is the "essay" question, which you answer in narrative form, used in civil service tests. Civil service tests are usually of the short-answer type. Full instructions for answering these questions will be given to you at the examination. But in case this is your first experience with short-answer questions and separate answer sheets, here is what you need to know:

1) Multiple-choice Questions
Most popular of the short-answer questions is the "multiple choice" or "best answer" question. It can be used, for example, to test for factual knowledge, ability to solve problems or judgment in meeting situations found at work.
A multiple-choice question is normally one of three types—
- It can begin with an incomplete statement followed by several possible endings. You are to find the one ending which *best* completes the statement, although some of the others may not be entirely wrong.
- It can also be a complete statement in the form of a question which is answered by choosing one of the statements listed.

- It can be in the form of a problem – again you select the best answer.

Here is an example of a multiple-choice question with a discussion which should give you some clues as to the method for choosing the right answer:

When an employee has a complaint about his assignment, the action which will *best* help him overcome his difficulty is to
  A. discuss his difficulty with his coworkers
  B. take the problem to the head of the organization
  C. take the problem to the person who gave him the assignment
  D. say nothing to anyone about his complaint

In answering this question, you should study each of the choices to find which is best. Consider choice "A" – Certainly an employee may discuss his complaint with fellow employees, but no change or improvement can result, and the complaint remains unresolved. Choice "B" is a poor choice since the head of the organization probably does not know what assignment you have been given, and taking your problem to him is known as "going over the head" of the supervisor. The supervisor, or person who made the assignment, is the person who can clarify it or correct any injustice. Choice "C" is, therefore, correct. To say nothing, as in choice "D," is unwise. Supervisors have and interest in knowing the problems employees are facing, and the employee is seeking a solution to his problem.

2) True/False Questions

The "true/false" or "right/wrong" form of question is sometimes used. Here a complete statement is given. Your job is to decide whether the statement is right or wrong.

SAMPLE: A roaming cell-phone call to a nearby city costs less than a non-roaming call to a distant city.

This statement is wrong, or false, since roaming calls are more expensive.

This is not a complete list of all possible question forms, although most of the others are variations of these common types. You will always get complete directions for answering questions. Be sure you understand *how* to mark your answers – ask questions until you do.

V. RECORDING YOUR ANSWERS

Computer terminals are used more and more today for many different kinds of exams.

For an examination with very few applicants, you may be told to record your answers in the test booklet itself. Separate answer sheets are much more common. If this separate answer sheet is to be scored by machine – and this is often the case – it is highly important that you mark your answers correctly in order to get credit.

An electronic scoring machine is often used in civil service offices because of the speed with which papers can be scored. Machine-scored answer sheets must be marked with a pencil, which will be given to you. This pencil has a high graphite content which responds to the electronic scoring machine. As a matter of fact, stray dots may register as answers, so do not let your pencil rest on the answer sheet while you are pondering the correct answer. Also, if your pencil lead breaks or is otherwise defective, ask for another.

Since the answer sheet will be dropped in a slot in the scoring machine, be careful not to bend the corners or get the paper crumpled.

The answer sheet normally has five vertical columns of numbers, with 30 numbers to a column. These numbers correspond to the question numbers in your test booklet. After each number, going across the page are four or five pairs of dotted lines. These short dotted lines have small letters or numbers above them. The first two pairs may also have a "T" or "F" above the letters. This indicates that the first two pairs only are to be used if the questions are of the true-false type. If the questions are multiple choice, disregard the "T" and "F" and pay attention only to the small letters or numbers.

Answer your questions in the manner of the sample that follows:

32. The largest city in the United States is
    A. Washington, D.C.
    B. New York City
    C. Chicago
    D. Detroit
    E. San Francisco

1) Choose the answer you think is best. (New York City is the largest, so "B" is correct.)
2) Find the row of dotted lines numbered the same as the question you are answering. (Find row number 32)
3) Find the pair of dotted lines corresponding to the answer. (Find the pair of lines under the mark "B.")
4) Make a solid black mark between the dotted lines.

VI. BEFORE THE TEST

Common sense will help you find procedures to follow to get ready for an examination. Too many of us, however, overlook these sensible measures. Indeed, nervousness and fatigue have been found to be the most serious reasons why applicants fail to do their best on civil service tests. Here is a list of reminders:

- Begin your preparation early – Don't wait until the last minute to go scurrying around for books and materials or to find out what the position is all about.
- Prepare continuously – An hour a night for a week is better than an all-night cram session. This has been definitely established. What is more, a night a week for a month will return better dividends than crowding your study into a shorter period of time.
- Locate the place of the exam – You have been sent a notice telling you when and where to report for the examination. If the location is in a different town or otherwise unfamiliar to you, it would be well to inquire the best route and learn something about the building.
- Relax the night before the test – Allow your mind to rest. Do not study at all that night. Plan some mild recreation or diversion; then go to bed early and get a good night's sleep.
- Get up early enough to make a leisurely trip to the place for the test – This way unforeseen events, traffic snarls, unfamiliar buildings, etc. will not upset you.
- Dress comfortably – A written test is not a fashion show. You will be known by number and not by name, so wear something comfortable.

- Leave excess paraphernalia at home – Shopping bags and odd bundles will get in your way. You need bring only the items mentioned in the official notice you received; usually everything you need is provided. Do not bring reference books to the exam. They will only confuse those last minutes and be taken away from you when in the test room.
- Arrive somewhat ahead of time – If because of transportation schedules you must get there very early, bring a newspaper or magazine to take your mind off yourself while waiting.
- Locate the examination room – When you have found the proper room, you will be directed to the seat or part of the room where you will sit. Sometimes you are given a sheet of instructions to read while you are waiting. Do not fill out any forms until you are told to do so; just read them and be prepared.
- Relax and prepare to listen to the instructions
- If you have any physical problem that may keep you from doing your best, be sure to tell the test administrator. If you are sick or in poor health, you really cannot do your best on the exam. You can come back and take the test some other time.

VII. AT THE TEST

The day of the test is here and you have the test booklet in your hand. The temptation to get going is very strong. Caution! There is more to success than knowing the right answers. You must know how to identify your papers and understand variations in the type of short-answer question used in this particular examination. Follow these suggestions for maximum results from your efforts:

1) Cooperate with the monitor

The test administrator has a duty to create a situation in which you can be as much at ease as possible. He will give instructions, tell you when to begin, check to see that you are marking your answer sheet correctly, and so on. He is not there to guard you, although he will see that your competitors do not take unfair advantage. He wants to help you do your best.

2) Listen to all instructions

Don't jump the gun! Wait until you understand all directions. In most civil service tests you get more time than you need to answer the questions. So don't be in a hurry. Read each word of instructions until you clearly understand the meaning. Study the examples, listen to all announcements and follow directions. Ask questions if you do not understand what to do.

3) Identify your papers

Civil service exams are usually identified by number only. You will be assigned a number; you must not put your name on your test papers. Be sure to copy your number correctly. Since more than one exam may be given, copy your exact examination title.

4) Plan your time

Unless you are told that a test is a "speed" or "rate of work" test, speed itself is usually not important. Time enough to answer all the questions will be provided, but this does not mean that you have all day. An overall time limit has been set. Divide the total time (in minutes) by the number of questions to determine the approximate time you have for each question.

5) Do not linger over difficult questions

If you come across a difficult question, mark it with a paper clip (useful to have along) and come back to it when you have been through the booklet. One caution if you do this – be sure to skip a number on your answer sheet as well. Check often to be sure that you have not lost your place and that you are marking in the row numbered the same as the question you are answering.

6) Read the questions

Be sure you know what the question asks! Many capable people are unsuccessful because they failed to *read* the questions correctly.

7) Answer all questions

Unless you have been instructed that a penalty will be deducted for incorrect answers, it is better to guess than to omit a question.

8) Speed tests

It is often better NOT to guess on speed tests. It has been found that on timed tests people are tempted to spend the last few seconds before time is called in marking answers at random – without even reading them – in the hope of picking up a few extra points. To discourage this practice, the instructions may warn you that your score will be "corrected" for guessing. That is, a penalty will be applied. The incorrect answers will be deducted from the correct ones, or some other penalty formula will be used.

9) Review your answers

If you finish before time is called, go back to the questions you guessed or omitted to give them further thought. Review other answers if you have time.

10) Return your test materials

If you are ready to leave before others have finished or time is called, take ALL your materials to the monitor and leave quietly. Never take any test material with you. The monitor can discover whose papers are not complete, and taking a test booklet may be grounds for disqualification.

VIII. EXAMINATION TECHNIQUES

1) Read the general instructions carefully. These are usually printed on the first page of the exam booklet. As a rule, these instructions refer to the timing of the examination; the fact that you should not start work until the signal and must stop work at a signal, etc. If there are any *special* instructions, such as a choice of questions to be answered, make sure that you note this instruction carefully.

2) When you are ready to start work on the examination, that is as soon as the signal has been given, read the instructions to each question booklet, underline any key words or phrases, such as *least, best, outline, describe* and the like. In this way you will tend to answer as requested rather than discover on reviewing your paper that you *listed without describing*, that you selected the *worst* choice rather than the *best* choice, etc.

3) If the examination is of the objective or multiple-choice type – that is, each question will also give a series of possible answers: A, B, C or D, and you are called upon to select the best answer and write the letter next to that answer on your answer paper – it is advisable to start answering each question in turn. There may be anywhere from 50 to 100 such questions in the three or four hours allotted and you can see how much time would be taken if you read through all the questions before beginning to answer any. Furthermore, if you come across a question or group of questions which you know would be difficult to answer, it would undoubtedly affect your handling of all the other questions.

4) If the examination is of the essay type and contains but a few questions, it is a moot point as to whether you should read all the questions before starting to answer any one. Of course, if you are given a choice – say five out of seven and the like – then it is essential to read all the questions so you can eliminate the two that are most difficult. If, however, you are asked to answer all the questions, there may be danger in trying to answer the easiest one first because you may find that you will spend too much time on it. The best technique is to answer the first question, then proceed to the second, etc.

5) Time your answers. Before the exam begins, write down the time it started, then add the time allowed for the examination and write down the time it must be completed, then divide the time available somewhat as follows:
   - If 3-1/2 hours are allowed, that would be 210 minutes. If you have 80 objective-type questions, that would be an average of 2-1/2 minutes per question. Allow yourself no more than 2 minutes per question, or a total of 160 minutes, which will permit about 50 minutes to review.
   - If for the time allotment of 210 minutes there are 7 essay questions to answer, that would average about 30 minutes a question. Give yourself only 25 minutes per question so that you have about 35 minutes to review.

6) The most important instruction is to *read each question* and make sure you know what is wanted. The second most important instruction is to *time yourself properly* so that you answer every question. The third most important instruction is to *answer every question*. Guess if you have to but include something for each question. Remember that you will receive no credit for a blank and will probably receive some credit if you write something in answer to an essay question. If you guess a letter – say "B" for a multiple-choice question – you may have guessed right. If you leave a blank as an answer to a multiple-choice question, the examiners may respect your feelings but it will not add a point to your score. Some exams may penalize you for wrong answers, so in such cases *only*, you may not want to guess unless you have some basis for your answer.

7) Suggestions
   a. Objective-type questions
      1. Examine the question booklet for proper sequence of pages and questions
      2. Read all instructions carefully
      3. Skip any question which seems too difficult; return to it after all other questions have been answered
      4. Apportion your time properly; do not spend too much time on any single question or group of questions

5. Note and underline key words – *all, most, fewest, least, best, worst, same, opposite,* etc.
6. Pay particular attention to negatives
7. Note unusual option, e.g., unduly long, short, complex, different or similar in content to the body of the question
8. Observe the use of "hedging" words – *probably, may, most likely,* etc.
9. Make sure that your answer is put next to the same number as the question
10. Do not second-guess unless you have good reason to believe the second answer is definitely more correct
11. Cross out original answer if you decide another answer is more accurate; do not erase until you are ready to hand your paper in
12. Answer all questions; guess unless instructed otherwise
13. Leave time for review

b. Essay questions
1. Read each question carefully
2. Determine exactly what is wanted. Underline key words or phrases.
3. Decide on outline or paragraph answer
4. Include many different points and elements unless asked to develop any one or two points or elements
5. Show impartiality by giving pros and cons unless directed to select one side only
6. Make and write down any assumptions you find necessary to answer the questions
7. Watch your English, grammar, punctuation and choice of words
8. Time your answers; don't crowd material

8) Answering the essay question

Most essay questions can be answered by framing the specific response around several key words or ideas. Here are a few such key words or ideas:

M's: manpower, materials, methods, money, management
P's: purpose, program, policy, plan, procedure, practice, problems, pitfalls, personnel, public relations

a. Six basic steps in handling problems:
1. Preliminary plan and background development
2. Collect information, data and facts
3. Analyze and interpret information, data and facts
4. Analyze and develop solutions as well as make recommendations
5. Prepare report and sell recommendations
6. Install recommendations and follow up effectiveness

b. Pitfalls to avoid
1. *Taking things for granted* – A statement of the situation does not necessarily imply that each of the elements is necessarily true; for example, a complaint may be invalid and biased so that all that can be taken for granted is that a complaint has been registered

2. *Considering only one side of a situation* – Wherever possible, indicate several alternatives and then point out the reasons you selected the best one
3. *Failing to indicate follow up* – Whenever your answer indicates action on your part, make certain that you will take proper follow-up action to see how successful your recommendations, procedures or actions turn out to be
4. *Taking too long in answering any single question* – Remember to time your answers properly

IX. AFTER THE TEST

Scoring procedures differ in detail among civil service jurisdictions although the general principles are the same. Whether the papers are hand-scored or graded by machine we have described, they are nearly always graded by number. That is, the person who marks the paper knows only the number – never the name – of the applicant. Not until all the papers have been graded will they be matched with names. If other tests, such as training and experience or oral interview ratings have been given, scores will be combined. Different parts of the examination usually have different weights. For example, the written test might count 60 percent of the final grade, and a rating of training and experience 40 percent. In many jurisdictions, veterans will have a certain number of points added to their grades.

After the final grade has been determined, the names are placed in grade order and an eligible list is established. There are various methods for resolving ties between those who get the same final grade – probably the most common is to place first the name of the person whose application was received first. Job offers are made from the eligible list in the order the names appear on it. You will be notified of your grade and your rank as soon as all these computations have been made. This will be done as rapidly as possible.

People who are found to meet the requirements in the announcement are called "eligibles." Their names are put on a list of eligible candidates. An eligible's chances of getting a job depend on how high he stands on this list and how fast agencies are filling jobs from the list.

When a job is to be filled from a list of eligibles, the agency asks for the names of people on the list of eligibles for that job. When the civil service commission receives this request, it sends to the agency the names of the three people highest on this list. Or, if the job to be filled has specialized requirements, the office sends the agency the names of the top three persons who meet these requirements from the general list.

The appointing officer makes a choice from among the three people whose names were sent to him. If the selected person accepts the appointment, the names of the others are put back on the list to be considered for future openings.

That is the rule in hiring from all kinds of eligible lists, whether they are for typist, carpenter, chemist, or something else. For every vacancy, the appointing officer has his choice of any one of the top three eligibles on the list. This explains why the person whose name is on top of the list sometimes does not get an appointment when some of the persons lower on the list do. If the appointing officer chooses the second or third eligible, the No. 1 eligible does not get a job at once, but stays on the list until he is appointed or the list is terminated.

X. HOW TO PASS THE INTERVIEW TEST

The examination for which you applied requires an oral interview test. You have already taken the written test and you are now being called for the interview test – the final part of the formal examination.

You may think that it is not possible to prepare for an interview test and that there are no procedures to follow during an interview. Our purpose is to point out some things you can do in advance that will help you and some good rules to follow and pitfalls to avoid while you are being interviewed.

What is an interview supposed to test?

The written examination is designed to test the technical knowledge and competence of the candidate; the oral is designed to evaluate intangible qualities, not readily measured otherwise, and to establish a list showing the relative fitness of each candidate – as measured against his competitors – for the position sought. Scoring is not on the basis of "right" and "wrong," but on a sliding scale of values ranging from "not passable" to "outstanding." As a matter of fact, it is possible to achieve a relatively low score without a single "incorrect" answer because of evident weakness in the qualities being measured.

Occasionally, an examination may consist entirely of an oral test – either an individual or a group oral. In such cases, information is sought concerning the technical knowledges and abilities of the candidate, since there has been no written examination for this purpose. More commonly, however, an oral test is used to supplement a written examination.

Who conducts interviews?

The composition of oral boards varies among different jurisdictions. In nearly all, a representative of the personnel department serves as chairman. One of the members of the board may be a representative of the department in which the candidate would work. In some cases, "outside experts" are used, and, frequently, a businessman or some other representative of the general public is asked to serve. Labor and management or other special groups may be represented. The aim is to secure the services of experts in the appropriate field.

However the board is composed, it is a good idea (and not at all improper or unethical) to ascertain in advance of the interview who the members are and what groups they represent. When you are introduced to them, you will have some idea of their backgrounds and interests, and at least you will not stutter and stammer over their names.

What should be done before the interview?

While knowledge about the board members is useful and takes some of the surprise element out of the interview, there is other preparation which is more substantive. It *is* possible to prepare for an oral interview – in several ways:

1) Keep a copy of your application and review it carefully before the interview

This may be the only document before the oral board, and the starting point of the interview. Know what education and experience you have listed there, and the sequence and dates of all of it. Sometimes the board will ask you to review the highlights of your experience for them; you should not have to hem and haw doing it.

2) Study the class specification and the examination announcement

Usually, the oral board has one or both of these to guide them. The qualities, characteristics or knowledges required by the position sought are stated in these documents. They offer valuable clues as to the nature of the oral interview. For example, if the job involves supervisory responsibilities, the announcement will usually indicate that knowledge of modern supervisory methods and the qualifications of the candidate as a supervisor will be tested. If so, you can expect such questions, frequently in the form of a hypothetical situation which you are expected to solve. NEVER go into an oral without knowledge of the duties and responsibilities of the job you seek.

3) Think through each qualification required

Try to visualize the kind of questions you would ask if you were a board member. How well could you answer them? Try especially to appraise your own knowledge and background in each area, *measured against the job sought*, and identify any areas in which you are weak. Be critical and realistic – do not flatter yourself.

4) Do some general reading in areas in which you feel you may be weak

For example, if the job involves supervision and your past experience has NOT, some general reading in supervisory methods and practices, particularly in the field of human relations, might be useful. Do NOT study agency procedures or detailed manuals. The oral board will be testing your understanding and capacity, not your memory.

5) Get a good night's sleep and watch your general health and mental attitude

You will want a clear head at the interview. Take care of a cold or any other minor ailment, and of course, no hangovers.

What should be done on the day of the interview?

Now comes the day of the interview itself. Give yourself plenty of time to get there. Plan to arrive somewhat ahead of the scheduled time, particularly if your appointment is in the fore part of the day. If a previous candidate fails to appear, the board might be ready for you a bit early. By early afternoon an oral board is almost invariably behind schedule if there are many candidates, and you may have to wait. Take along a book or magazine to read, or your application to review, but leave any extraneous material in the waiting room when you go in for your interview. In any event, relax and compose yourself.

The matter of dress is important. The board is forming impressions about you – from your experience, your manners, your attitude, and your appearance. Give your personal appearance careful attention. Dress your best, but not your flashiest. Choose conservative, appropriate clothing, and be sure it is immaculate. This is a business interview, and your appearance should indicate that you regard it as such. Besides, being well groomed and properly dressed will help boost your confidence.

Sooner or later, someone will call your name and escort you into the interview room. *This is it.* From here on you are on your own. It is too late for any more preparation. But remember, you asked for this opportunity to prove your fitness, and you are here because your request was granted.

What happens when you go in?

The usual sequence of events will be as follows: The clerk (who is often the board stenographer) will introduce you to the chairman of the oral board, who will introduce you to the other members of the board. Acknowledge the introductions before you sit down. Do not be surprised if you find a microphone facing you or a stenotypist sitting by. Oral interviews are usually recorded in the event of an appeal or other review.

Usually the chairman of the board will open the interview by reviewing the highlights of your education and work experience from your application – primarily for the benefit of the other members of the board, as well as to get the material into the record. Do not interrupt or comment unless there is an error or significant misinterpretation; if that is the case, do not hesitate. But do not quibble about insignificant matters. Also, he will usually ask you some question about your education, experience or your present job – partly to get you to start talking and to establish the interviewing "rapport." He may start the actual questioning, or turn it over to one of the other members. Frequently, each member undertakes the questioning on a particular area, one in which he is perhaps most competent, so you can expect each member to participate in the examination. Because time is limited, you may also expect some rather abrupt switches in the direction the questioning takes, so do not be upset by it. Normally, a board member will not pursue a single line of questioning unless he discovers a particular strength or weakness.

After each member has participated, the chairman will usually ask whether any member has any further questions, then will ask you if you have anything you wish to add. Unless you are expecting this question, it may floor you. Worse, it may start you off on an extended, extemporaneous speech. The board is not usually seeking more information. The question is principally to offer you a last opportunity to present further qualifications or to indicate that you have nothing to add. So, if you feel that a significant qualification or characteristic has been overlooked, it is proper to point it out in a sentence or so. Do not compliment the board on the thoroughness of their examination – they have been sketchy, and you know it. If you wish, merely say, "No thank you, I have nothing further to add." This is a point where you can "talk yourself out" of a good impression or fail to present an important bit of information. Remember, *you close the interview yourself*.

The chairman will then say, "That is all, Mr. _____, thank you." Do not be startled; the interview is over, and quicker than you think. Thank him, gather your belongings and take your leave. Save your sigh of relief for the other side of the door.

How to put your best foot forward

Throughout this entire process, you may feel that the board individually and collectively is trying to pierce your defenses, seek out your hidden weaknesses and embarrass and confuse you. Actually, this is not true. They are obliged to make an appraisal of your qualifications for the job you are seeking, and they want to see you in your best light. Remember, they must interview all candidates and a non-cooperative candidate may become a failure in spite of their best efforts to bring out his qualifications. Here are 15 suggestions that will help you:

1) Be natural – Keep your attitude confident, not cocky

If you are not confident that you can do the job, do not expect the board to be. Do not apologize for your weaknesses, try to bring out your strong points. The board is interested in a positive, not negative, presentation. Cockiness will antagonize any board member and make him wonder if you are covering up a weakness by a false show of strength.

2) Get comfortable, but don't lounge or sprawl

Sit erectly but not stiffly. A careless posture may lead the board to conclude that you are careless in other things, or at least that you are not impressed by the importance of the occasion. Either conclusion is natural, even if incorrect. Do not fuss with your clothing, a pencil or an ashtray. Your hands may occasionally be useful to emphasize a point; do not let them become a point of distraction.

3) Do not wisecrack or make small talk

This is a serious situation, and your attitude should show that you consider it as such. Further, the time of the board is limited – they do not want to waste it, and neither should you.

4) Do not exaggerate your experience or abilities

In the first place, from information in the application or other interviews and sources, the board may know more about you than you think. Secondly, you probably will not get away with it. An experienced board is rather adept at spotting such a situation, so do not take the chance.

5) If you know a board member, do not make a point of it, yet do not hide it

Certainly you are not fooling him, and probably not the other members of the board. Do not try to take advantage of your acquaintanceship – it will probably do you little good.

6) Do not dominate the interview

Let the board do that. They will give you the clues – do not assume that you have to do all the talking. Realize that the board has a number of questions to ask you, and do not try to take up all the interview time by showing off your extensive knowledge of the answer to the first one.

7) Be attentive

You only have 20 minutes or so, and you should keep your attention at its sharpest throughout. When a member is addressing a problem or question to you, give him your undivided attention. Address your reply principally to him, but do not exclude the other board members.

8) Do not interrupt

A board member may be stating a problem for you to analyze. He will ask you a question when the time comes. Let him state the problem, and wait for the question.

9) Make sure you understand the question

Do not try to answer until you are sure what the question is. If it is not clear, restate it in your own words or ask the board member to clarify it for you. However, do not haggle about minor elements.

10) Reply promptly but not hastily

A common entry on oral board rating sheets is "candidate responded readily," or "candidate hesitated in replies." Respond as promptly and quickly as you can, but do not jump to a hasty, ill-considered answer.

11) Do not be peremptory in your answers

A brief answer is proper – but do not fire your answer back. That is a losing game from your point of view. The board member can probably ask questions much faster than you can answer them.

12) Do not try to create the answer you think the board member wants

He is interested in what kind of mind you have and how it works – not in playing games. Furthermore, he can usually spot this practice and will actually grade you down on it.

13) Do not switch sides in your reply merely to agree with a board member

Frequently, a member will take a contrary position merely to draw you out and to see if you are willing and able to defend your point of view. Do not start a debate, yet do not surrender a good position. If a position is worth taking, it is worth defending.

14) Do not be afraid to admit an error in judgment if you are shown to be wrong

The board knows that you are forced to reply without any opportunity for careful consideration. Your answer may be demonstrably wrong. If so, admit it and get on with the interview.

15) Do not dwell at length on your present job

The opening question may relate to your present assignment. Answer the question but do not go into an extended discussion. You are being examined for a *new* job, not your present one. As a matter of fact, try to phrase ALL your answers in terms of the job for which you are being examined.

Basis of Rating

Probably you will forget most of these "do's" and "don'ts" when you walk into the oral interview room. Even remembering them all will not ensure you a passing grade. Perhaps you did not have the qualifications in the first place. But remembering them will help you to put your best foot forward, without treading on the toes of the board members.

Rumor and popular opinion to the contrary notwithstanding, an oral board wants you to make the best appearance possible. They know you are under pressure – but they also want to see how you respond to it as a guide to what your reaction would be under the pressures of the job you seek. They will be influenced by the degree of poise you display, the personal traits you show and the manner in which you respond.

ABOUT THIS BOOK

This book contains tests divided into Examination Sections. Go through each test, answering every question in the margin. We have also attached a sample answer sheet at the back of the book that can be removed and used. At the end of each test look at the answer key and check your answers. On the ones you got wrong, look at the right answer choice and learn. Do not fill in the answers first. Do not memorize the questions and answers, but understand the answer and principles involved. On your test, the questions will likely be different from the samples. Questions are changed and new ones added. If you understand these past questions you should have success with any changes that arise. Tests may consist of several types of questions. We have additional books on each subject should more study be advisable or necessary for you. Finally, the more you study, the better prepared you will be. This book is intended to be the last thing you study before you walk into the examination room. Prior study of relevant texts is also recommended. NLC publishes some of these in our Fundamental Series. Knowledge and good sense are important factors in passing your exam. Good luck also helps. So now study this Passbook, absorb the material contained within and take that knowledge into the examination. Then do your best to pass that exam.

EXAMINATION SECTION

EXAMINATION SECTION
TEST 1

DIRECTIONS: Each question or incomplete statement is followed by several suggested, answers or completions. Select the one that BEST answers the question or completes the statement. *PRINT THE LETTER OF THE CORRECT ANSWER IN THE SPACE AT THE RIGHT.*

1. The authority to establish zoning ordinances by a community comes from

    A. the police power of the state
    B. local determination
    C. the federal government
    D. implied powers of the community

    1.____

2. On a land use map, the standard color used to designate residential use is

    A. green   B. blue   C. purple   D. yellow

    2.____

3. In population analysis, a population pyramid indicates

    A. male and female age groupings
    B. total population projections
    C. fertility ratios
    D. educational achievements

    3.____

4. The determination of a standard metropolitan statistical area is established by

    A. local considerations   B. regional agencies
    C. the U.S. Census Bureau   D. state agencies

    4.____

5. The population census of the United States is taken every _____ years.

    A. 2   B. 4   C. 5   D. 10

    5.____

6. There are strong indications that planning agencies are developing a new approach to the traditional methods of city planning.
   This new approach is called

    A. advocacy planning
    B. long-range physical planning
    C. community development
    D. policies planning

    6.____

7. A key element of a comprehensive plan for a community is the

    A. zoning ordinance   B. land use plan
    C. official map   D. subdivision regulation

    7.____

8. The official map of a community is a document that

    A. shows population projections and educational trends
    B. pinpoints the location of future streets and other public facilities
    C. identifies capital improvements and budgets
    D. indicates all community facilities

    8.____

9. During the past decade, planning programs generally have become increasingly concerned with which one of the following?

   A. Long-range physical design
   B. Highway locations
   C. Social welfare
   D. Natural resources

10. The city planning process encompasses several basic phases. Which one of the following phases would NOT be considered typical?

    A. Cost-benefit analysis
    B. Goal formulation
    C. Data collection and research
    D. Plan preparation and programming

11. The MOST common use of easements in new housing subdivisions is for

    A. air rights   B. utilities
    C. open space   D. absorption fields

12. The phrase *non-complying use* relates to which one of the following regulations?

    A. Zoning Ordinance   B. Building Code
    C. Subdivision regulations   D. Health Code

13. Performance standards are generally associated with which one of the following types of zoning districts?

    A. Residential   B. Commercial
    C. Manufacturing   D. Flood plain

14. The PRIMARY goal of cluster-type development is to

    A. increase population density
    B. insure open space
    C. discourage rapid development
    D. bypass zoning requirements

15. Which of the following is MOST closely related to the land-use intensity standards developed by the Federal Housing Administration?

    A. Quality of housing   B. Planned unit development
    C. Low-cost housing   D. Land management policy

16. If the density of a residential subdivision is 8 dwelling units per acre, then the average size lot should be APPROXIMATELY

    A. 25 ft. x 100 ft.   B. 55 ft. x 100 ft.
    C. 100 ft. x 100 ft.   D. 200 ft. x 200 ft.

17. In planning the open parking area for community facilities, the amount of space allocated per care should be APPROXIMATELY _____ sq.ft.

    A. 150   B. 300   C. 600   D. 800

18. Which of the following facilities would be MOST appropriate on the roof of a building? 18.____

    A. Stolport B. Heliport
    C. Airport D. Cargo port

19. Sanitary landfill is a method of 19.____

    A. sewage disposal B. composting
    C. incineration D. refuse disposal

20. Which of the following is NOT considered to be an air pollutant by the Environmental Protection Agency? 20.____

    A. Nitrates B. Sulfur oxides
    C. Carbon monoxide D. Hydrocarbons

21. Which of the following recreation facilities is NOT considered a typical neighborhood facility? 21.____

    A. Tot lot B. Playground
    C. Wading pool D. Playfield

22. Which of the following methods would be the MOST accurate in making a population projection for a small community? 22.____

    A. Migration and natural increase
    B. Apportionment and voting records
    C. School enrollment and housing starts
    D. Geometric extrapolation

23. When a planning map is to be reproduced to different sizes, the map scale should be expressed 23.____

    A. mathematically B. in graphic form
    C. in feet and inches D. by metes and bounds

24. The one of the following characteristics which is NOT typical of new industrial parks is 24.____

    A. off-street loading B. extensive landscaping
    C. employee parking D. 2-story structures

25. A greenbelt surrounding a community can be used for many activities. The one of the following activities LEAST appropriate for greenbelt use is 25.____

    A. farming B. recreation
    C. local shopping D. flood plain control

KEY (CORRECT ANSWERS)

1. A
2. D
3. A
4. C
5. D

6. D
7. B
8. B
9. C
10. A

11. B
12. A
13. C
14. B
15. B

16. B
17. B
18. B
19. D
20. A

21. D
22. A
23. B
24. D
25. C

TEST 2

DIRECTIONS: Each question or incomplete statement is followed by several suggested answers or completions. Select the one that BEST answers the question or completes the statement. *PRINT THE LETTER OF THE CORRECT ANSWER IN THE SPACE AT THE RIGHT.*

1. The *neighborhood unit* concept does NOT provide for

   A. elementary schools B. playgrounds
   C. local shopping D. industrial development

   1.____

2. Which of the following areas is LEAST likely to be considered part of social welfare planning?

   A. Urban design B. Education
   C. Health D. Anti-poverty

   2.____

3. Both the census of business and the census of manufacturing compiled by the U.S. Bureau of the Census are made every _____ years.

   A. three B. five C. seven D. ten

   3.____

4. The MOST frequently used governmental source for topographical maps is the U.S.

   A. Department of Agriculture
   B. Geological Survey
   C. Department of Housing and Urban Development
   D. Coast Guard

   4.____

5. The importance of assessed valuation of land and buildings to a community is to

   A. establish school taxes
   B. establish property taxes
   C. determine tax exemptions
   D. determine land uses

   5.____

6. Of the following countries, the MOST extensive progress in establishing new towns during the 20th century has taken place in

   A. the United States B. France
   C. Italy D. England

   6.____

7. A street classification system is PRIMARILY used for street

   A. naming B. construction
   C. differentiation D. location

   7.____

8. The *Greenbelt* towns were a product of the

   A. city beautiful movement
   B. garden city movement
   C. atomic energy commission
   D. resettlement administration

   8.____

9. The apportionment method of population projection is concerned PRIMARILY with

   A. migration
   B. natural increase
   C. large geographic areas
   D. birth rate

10. Under ideal conditions, which type of parking arrangement should yield the MOST parking spaces?

    A. Parallel   B. 45°   C. 60°   D. 90°

11. A MAJOR disadvantage of a depressed highway through a built-up area as compared to a highway on grade is its

    A. poor appearance
    B. inadequate width of right-of-way
    C. lack of access
    D. noise generation

12. The customary test made to determine the ability of a soil to drain off liquids, such as those discharged by a cesspool, is known as the _____ test.

    A. percolation
    B. absorption
    C. drainage
    D. sump

13. The Mitchell-Lama Housing Law was originally intended to assist the construction of

    A. low-income housing
    B. middle-income housing
    C. suburban residential projects
    D. housing for mixed racial communities

14. A community will MOST frequently acquire the development rights of existing farm land in order to

    A. protect land values
    B. provide sites for public projects
    C. insure open space
    D. develop a land bank

15. In recent years, local participation in the city planning process has *substantially* increased because of the

    A. establishment of local school boards
    B. high crime rate in the streets
    C. emergence of private citizen organizations
    D. establishment of community planning boards

16. A unique feature of the State Urban Development Corporation when first established was that it

    A. was an autonomous organization
    B. was not required to conform to local zoning regulations
    C. could only build housing when invited by local communities
    D. used only private funds for its projects

17. The concept of *defensible space* has recently emerged to help fight crime in urban areas. The principle of *defensible space* is that public areas should be

    A. completely enclosed
    B. eliminated
    C. placed adjacent to areas of activity
    D. patroled by volunteer citizen groups

17.____

18. Of the following, the MAJOR planning implication of a 3-bedroom dwelling unit as compared to a 1-bedroom dwelling unit is that

    A. the family with the larger dwelling unit has more income
    B. with larger dwelling units there will be fewer municipal services necessary
    C. more children will be enrolled in school
    D. smaller dwelling units are cheaper to build than larger units

18.____

19. A landscaped buffer strip is MOST appropriately placed between which of the following land uses?

    A. Light and heavy manufacturing
    B. Residential and commercial
    C. Commercial and manufacturing
    D. Residential of low density and residential of high density

19.____

20. The employment trend in the city over the past 20 years has shown that

    A. *both* white collar and blue collar jobs have increased
    B. *both* white collar and blue collar jobs have decreased
    C. *only* white collar jobs have decreased
    D. *only* blue collar jobs have decreased

20.____

21. For traffic safety, the BEST angle between two intersecting streets is

    A. 15   B. 30   C. 45   D. 90

21.____

22. In the city, the system used by the tax department to identify property is by

    A. house numbers   B. zoning maps
    C. block and lot numbers   D. the official city map

22.____

23. The name of the report by which the U.S. Environmental Protection Agency establishes the effect of a proposed project on the environment is called the

    A. input-output analysis   B. economic base study
    C. ambient air study   D. impact statement

23.____

24. Planners recommend that utility lines be located underground because utility lines built this way are

    A. cheaper to construct
    B. not required to follow street alignments
    C. aesthetically more attractive
    D. more efficient

24.____

25. *Scatter-site* housing means that the housing will be
    A. located in all use districts
    B. built with large areas of recreation space between buildings
    C. of different heights on each site
    D. built on small, by-passed sites in built-up areas

KEY (CORRECT ANSWERS)

1. D	11. C
2. A	12. A
3. B	13. B
4. B	14. C
5. B	15. D
6. D	16. B
7. C	17. C
8. D	18. C
9. C	19. B
10. D	20. D

21. D
22. C
23. D
24. C
25. D

EXAMINATION SECTION
TEST 1

DIRECTIONS: Each question or incomplete statement is followed by several suggested answers or completions. Select the one that BEST answers the questions or completes the statement. *PRINT THE LETTER OF THE CORRECT ANSWER IN THE SPACE AT THE RIGHT.*

1. Of the following, the FIRST operation in the demolition of a 4-story building adjacent to the property line is the

    A. erection of railings around the stairwells
    B. shoring of adjoining buildings
    C. erection of a sidewalk shed
    D. removal of windows

    1.____

2. Projected sash is defined as a(n)

    A. double hung window
    B. window that opens inward or outward
    C. architectural projection from a building exterior
    D. storm window

    2.____

3. Specifications for a reinforced concrete structure call for a roof fill to be placed on the concrete roof slab. Of the following, the PURPOSE of the fill is to

    A. reduce sound transmission
    B. facilitate drainage
    C. provide a smooth base for insulation
    D. protect the concrete slab

    3.____

4. The Building Department requires a location survey by a licensed surveyor

    A. *only* if it is suspected that the building is not in the proper place and may impinge on adjacent property
    B. *only* of the completed foundation
    C. *only* of the completed superstructure
    D. *after* the foundation is completed and a second survey after the building is completed

    4.____

5. After excavating by a contractor for a footing, the sub-grade soil appears to be below the quality shown on the borings.
   Of the following types of footings, the one that would be LEAST affected by this condition is a

    A. spread footing   B. combined footing
    C. footing on piles   D. footing and pier

    5.____

6. Of the following, the information of GREATEST significance to be recorded for each pile during pile driving is the

    A. steam pressure and the temperature
    B. condition of the ground at the pile location

    6.____

9

C. number of hammer blows at the last inch
D. total number of hammer blows

7. One method of dewatering an excavation for a foundation is by the use of

   A. inverted siphons
   B. well points
   C. line holes
   D. suction heads

8. An excavation for a concrete footing to support a structural steel column was dug 4" too deep.
   Of the following, the BEST construction practice would be to

   A. backfill the 4" with stone
   B. backfill the 4" with sand
   C. lower the entire footing 4"
   D. make the footing 4" thicker

9. Spudding, in a pile driving operation, is used PRIMARILY to

   A. remove a broken pile
   B. pass an obstruction
   C. compact the soil in the area
   D. splice piles

10. Where walers and form ties are used in wood formwork for tall vertical concrete walls, the walers are

    A. more closely spaced at the top of the wall than at the bottom
    B. evenly spaced at the top to the bottom of the wall
    C. more closely spaced at the bottom of the wall than at the top
    D. more closely spaced at the middle of the wall than at either the top or the bottom

11. A non-bearing wall unit between columns enclosing a structure is known as a _____ wall.

    A. panel
    B. curtain
    C. apron
    D. spandrel

12. In a multi-story building, standpipes are installed FIRST by the plumber for

    A. water supply
    B. sanitary facilities
    C. fire protection
    D. steam supply

13. It is necessary to burn reinforcing steel while they are in the wood forms in order to change their lengths.
    The STANDARD safety precaution to observe during this process is to

    A. fireproof the wood forms
    B. use a low heat flame
    C. have a man stand by with a fire extinguisher
    D. soak a 20-foot radius around the area with water

14. Specifications for a building require that the first floor beams must be in place before backfilling against the foundation walls.
    Of the following, the BEST reason for this requirement is that

    A. the utilities up to the first floor level should be in place before backfilling
    B. without the first floor beams in place, the wall may become overstressed
    C. it facilitates the inspection of the first floor construction
    D. it facilitates the inspection of the backfilling operation

15. The utility line that USUALLY enters the building at the *lowest* elevation is the

    A. electric cable
    B. gas lines
    C. water lines
    D. plumbing drain

16. Specifications for a building require that machine excavation for foundation footings be within a foot of final subgrade and the remaining excavation be done by hand. Of the following, the BEST reasons for this requirement is to

    A. prevent cave-ins around the excavation
    B. save the amount of fill needed
    C. prevent disturbing the surrounding excavation
    D. prevent excavation below the subgrade

17. Of the following outside lines entering a building, the one for which grades must be MOST carefully controlled is the

    A. sewer line
    B. water line
    C. gas line
    D. electric cable

18. On a plan, the grades for a building are as follows:
    Datum ± 0 (Elev. 24.08')
    First floor El + 1' - 0" (Elev. 25.08').
    The elevation of a ledge 6'3" below the finished first floor level with respect to datum is

    A. El. - 6.25
    B. El. - 5.25
    C. El. + 18.83
    D. El. + 17.83

19. Specifications for a building call for *defective material to be removed from the job site immediately*. The MAIN reason for this is to

    A. prevent accidents
    B. prevent accidental use of the defective material in the construction
    C. insure that the contractor does not make the same mistake again
    D. minimize claims against the department

20. *Drywall* is installed by

    A. carpenters
    B. lathers
    C. plasterers
    D. masons

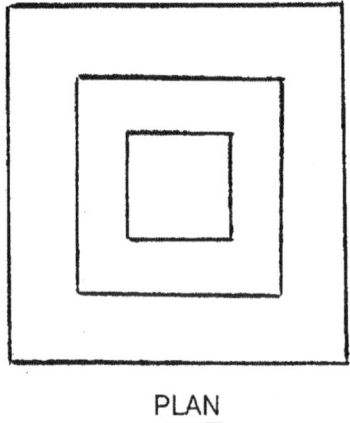

PLAN

21. The Plan of a footing and concrete column is shown above. An elevation of the footing would be shown as: 21.____

A. 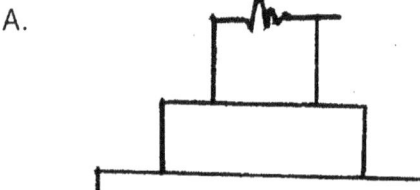   B.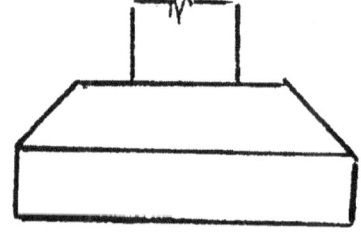

C. 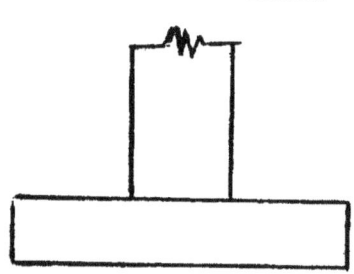   D.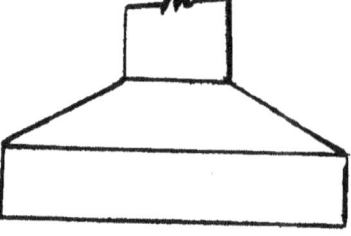

22. Of the following, the BEST sequence to follow in pouring the interior footing, concrete column and basement floor as shown below is pour the footing, 22.____

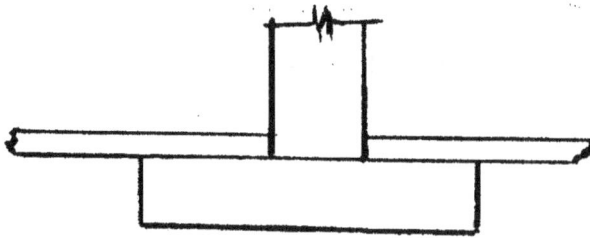

    A. and floor in one pour. Pour the column
    B. and column in one pour. Pour the floor
    C. pour the floor above the footing, pour the column above the floor
    D. box out for the floor, pour the column. Pour the floor

23. The PURPOSE of curing concrete is so that the   23.____

    A. forms for the concrete can be stripped quickly
    B. water content will not evaporate too quickly
    C. concrete will harden faster
    D. reinforcing rods will not rust

24. Air-entraining cement may be required so that the resulting concrete will resist   24.____

    A. freezing and thawing   B. hot weather
    C. dampness   D. heavy loads

25. Concrete test cylinders are required to   25.____

    A. provide an indication of the strength of the concrete poured in a specific location
    B. provide a basis of payment
    C. check on the inspector
    D. check the source of material

26. Concrete test cylinders are stored and cured on the job   26.____

    A. so that the contractor can then control the curing
    B. so that the inspector can then control the curing
    C. because the laboratory has no facilities for curing concrete cylinders
    D. because conditions of curing on the job are the same as at the location poured

27. The *water-cement ratio* refers to the quantity of water in a concrete mix as   27.____

    A. cubic feet of water per cubic foot of cement
    B. gallons of water per pound of cement
    C. gallons of water per sack of cement
    D. bags of cement per gallon of water

28. *Slump* of concrete refers to the   28.____

    A. shrinkage of concrete while setting
    B. drop in height relative to a standard testing cone
    C. amount of water introduced into the concrete
    D. cracking or crazing of the surface of concrete

29. Concrete mixes made with lightweight aggregate USUALLY require the addition of an air-entraining agent in order to   29.____

    A. increase the strength of the concrete
    B. reduce the weight of the concrete
    C. obtain the necessary plasticity without added water
    D. save aggregate material

30. Concrete in some instances requires integral waterproofing.   30.____
    This can BEST be achieved by

    A. addition of more cement in the mix
    B. longer vibration
    C. addition of a waterproofing agent to the mix
    D. longer curing period

31. In placing concrete where the vertical drop is greater than 5 feet, the use of an elephant trunk is necessary.
The BEST reason for using an elephant trunk is to

    A. prevent segregation of the aggregate
    B. prevent waste of material
    C. safeguard health and property
    D. save time and labor

32. According to the Building Code, the maximum size of coarse aggregate for reinforced concrete shall be one-fifth of the narrowest dimension between forms or three-quarters of the clear spacing between reinforcing bars. Of the following, the MAXIMUM sized aggregate permitted for a 12" wall with #6 bars spaced at 3" center to center is

    A. 1 3/4"   B. 1 1/2"   C. 1 1/4"   D. 1"

33. Of the following, the one that is NOT a name for a lightweight aggregate is

    A. Solite   B. Vitralite
    C. Lelite   D. Nitralite

34. High early strength cement is designated as

    A. Type I   B. Type II   C. Type III   D. Type IV

35. The average weight of stone concrete is, MOST NEARLY, _____ lb./cu. ft.

    A. 125   B. 150
    C. 175   D. 200

KEY (CORRECT ANSWERS)

1.	C	16.	D
2.	B	17.	A
3.	B	18.	B
4.	D	19.	B
5.	C	20.	A
6.	C	21.	A
7.	B	22.	D
8.	D	23.	B
9.	B	24.	A
10.	C	25.	A
11.	B	26.	D
12.	C	27.	C
13.	C	28.	B
14.	B	29.	C
15.	D	30.	C

31. A
32. B
33. B
34. C
35. B

TEST 2

DIRECTIONS: Each question or incomplete statement is followed by several suggested answers or completions. Select the one that BEST answers the question or completes the statement. *PRINT THE LETTER OF THE CORRECT ANSWER IN THE SPACE AT THE RIGHT.*

1. The Building Code requires that concrete shall be kept in a moist condition, after placing, for at least the FIRST _____ days.

    A. 3   B. 7   C. 14   D. 28

2. In concrete work, a dummy joint is SIMILAR in purpose to a(n) _____ joint.

    A. expansion   B. construction
    C. contraction   D. shear

3. Specifications for concrete usually contain a statement disallowing the *retampering* of concrete. *Retampering* means

    A. adding more water to the drum after ingredients are mixed
    B. vibrating of concrete in the forms
    C. mixing of the remaining concrete after some concrete is taken from the truck
    D. mixing of concrete in the truck after it has partially set and adding water

4. Chamfers are placed on a concrete beam PRIMARILY to

    A. save weight   B. eliminate honeycomb
    C. eliminate sharp corners D. save construction costs

5. Of the following, the BEST reason for using vibrators in concrete construction is to

    A. increase the workability of the concrete
    B. consolidate the concrete
    C. slow up the setting
    D. speed up the setting

6. The concrete test that will BEST determine the consistency of a concrete mix is the

    A. sieve analysis   B. water-cement ratio test
    C. calorimetric test   D. slump test

7. Specifications for the concrete floor treatment of a building require *dustproofing*. This process consists of

    A. scraping the floor surface to remove loose concrete material that will dust
    B. mopping the floor with a chemical solution that will harden the concrete surface
    C. adding a chemical compound to the concrete mix that will harden the surface of the concrete
    D. grinding the concrete floor with a terrazzo machine that will case harden the surface of the concrete

8. In checking the placement of reinforcing steel, it is discovered that reinforcing steel called for on the design drawings is not shown on the reinforcing steel shop drawings. Of the following, the BEST procedure to follow is to

A. check the design drawings for the errors
B. check the shop drawings for the errors
C. subtract the missing steel in the field
D. stop all work

9. While a large spread footing of about 50 cubic yards Is being poured, the supply plant breaks down. Concrete is available from another supplier.
The use of the other supplier should

   A. not be approved because the supplier may not be approved
   B. be approved since additional test cylinders can be taken
   C. not be approved since construction joints can be installed where the pour has ended
   D. be approved as the concrete in footings is relatively unimportant

9.____

10. Of the following species of lumber, the one MOST likely to be used for concrete formwork is

    A. oak   B. pine   C. maple   D. birch

10.____

11. A contractor proposes to install the roofing two days after the concrete roof slab is poured.
This proposal should

    A. *be recommended* as it will speed the construction
    B. *be recommended* as it will cure the concrete better
    C. *not be recommended* as excess water may bulge the roofing
    D. *not be recommended* in cold weather but would be recommended in warm weather

11.____

12. For the construction of concrete floors resting on earth, the item that should be MOST carefully checked is that

    A. the earth is dry before pouring
    B. the earth is wet before pouring
    C. all backfill is properly compacted
    D. all backfill is porous soil

12.____

13. Cracks in concrete are not necessarily caused by settlement of a structure. Sometimes they are caused by

    A. shrinkage   B. plastic flow
    C. hydration   D. curing

13.____

14. Specifications for a building state that reinforcing bars must lap 40 diameters in the concrete.
The length of lap for a number 6 bar should be, MOST NEARLY, _____ inches.

    A. 12   B. 20   C. 30   D. 40

14.____

15. Cement stored on the job site that has become caked and lumpy may

    A. be used only for foundations
    B. be used only for slabs on ground
    C. be used anywhere if the lumps are broken up
    D. not be used

15.____

16. Of the following statements relating to the plies in plywood, the one that is CORRECT is:
    A. The primary difference between exterior and interior plywood is the quality of the exterior plies.
    B. Exterior plywood has more plies than interior plywood.
    C. Exterior plywood has no surface defects on the outer plies while interior plywood permits surface defects on the outer plies.
    D. Plywood has an odd number of plies.

17. Of the following, the one that is NOT a principal classification of lumber according to the American Lumber Standards is
    A. building   B. structural
    C. yard   D. shop

18. Of the following types of lumber, the one that is classified as a hardwood is
    A. cedar   B. fir   C. pine   D. maple

19. When building the formwork for a 12" doubly reinforced concrete wall, the USUAL order of conctruction is to place the
    A. formwork for both faces of the wall; then place the steel
    B. formwork for one face of the wall, place all reinforcing steel, then place the formwork for the other face of the wall
    C. reinforcing steel, then place the formwork for both faces of the wall
    D. formwork for one face of the wall, place the reinforcing steel for one face, place the form-work for the other face of the wall, then place the reinforcing steel for the second face

20. To obtain information concerning the product of a particular major manufacturer of flooring, the BEST of the following sources of information is the
    A. Architectural Standards   B. ASTM
    C. Sweet's Catalogue   D. Flooring Institute

21. Of the following, loose lintels would MOST likely be found in the specifications under the item entitled
    A. Ornamental Iron   B. Miscellaneous Iron
    C. Structural Steel   D. Hollow Metal Work

22. Galvanized metal lath is metal lath coated with
    A. tin   B. copper   C. zinc   D. nickel

23. In the welding symbol the 2 represents the
    A. spacing between welds in inches
    B. length of the weld in inches
    C. number of sides to be welded
    D. thickness of the throat of the weld in inches

24. The specification for a building states that rib lath should be 3.4 pounds. 24.____
This MEANS 3.4 pounds per

   A. square foot
   B. linear foot of a 3 foot roll
   C. square yard
   D. 10 square feet

25. Terrazzo floors are laid with brass dividing strips PRIMARILY for the purpose of 25.____

   A. preventing slipping
   B. appearance
   C. preventing irregular cracking
   D. easy screeding

26. The PURPOSE of a chase is to 26.____

   A. support stair stringers
   B. accomodate pipes in a wall
   C. accomodate flashing in a parapet
   D. provide venting

27. In masonry work, a bull nose brick would be located at 27.____

   A. an inside corner   B. an outside corner
   C. the key of an arch   D. the roof of a boiler setting

28. The addition of lime to cement mortar improves the workability of mortar and 28.____

   A. increases the strength
   B. decreases the shrinkage
   C. decreases the weight
   D. increases the watertightness

29. Brickwork must be cleaned after completion of setting by 29.____

   A. scrubbing with soap solution and water
   B. wire brushing
   C. washing with muriatic solution
   D. sand blasting

30. In a multi-story building, weep holes in cavity wall brick construction are USUALLY 30.____
placed in the brickwork

   A. above all masonry openings
   B. at foundation level only
   C. at the parapet only
   D. at every floor

31. A brick wall which consists of all stretcher courses is said to be built with a _____ Bond. 31.____

   A. Flemish   B. Running
   C. English   D. Common

32. The whitish deposit frequently seen on brick walls can USUALLY be avoided by

   A. using brick that contains more soluable salts
   B. keeping the water-mortar ratio high
   C. adding muriatic acid to the mortar
   D. constructing properly filled weathertight joints

33. Specifications for a building require brick to be wet before using.
Of the following, the BEST reason for this requirement is that wetting

   A. makes it easier to place brick
   B. cleans the brick
   C. prevents absorption of moisture from the mortar
   D. shows up flaws in the brick that would otherwise be hidden

34. In checking the ingredients that are to go into the concrete for a footing that is being poured, you notice that there is 5% too much cement.
Of the following, the BEST action to take in this situation is to

   A. do nothing
   B. condemn the footing
   C. increase the amount of sand in the mix
   D. order core borings taken of the finished footing

35. The soil conditions for a new building are MOST frequently checked by

   A. augering   B. soundings
   C. rodding   D. borings

KEY (CORRECT ANSWERS)

1. B
2. C
3. D
4. C
5. B

6. D
7. B
8. B
9. B
10. B

11. C
12. C
13. A
14. C
15. D

16. D
17. A
18. D
19. B
20. C

21. B
22. C
23. B
24. C
25. C

26. B
27. B
28. B
29. C
30. D

31. B
32. D
33. C
34. A
35. D

EXAMINATION SECTION
TEST 1

DIRECTIONS: Each question or incomplete statement is followed by several suggested answers or completions. Select the one that BEST answers the question or completes the statement. *PRINT THE LETTER OF THE CORRECT ANSWER IN THE SPACE AT THE RIGHT.*

1. When a sidewalk shed is required in connection with the erection of a building, the Code provides that the shed must be completed before the building has risen to a height, in feet, of

    A. 12   B. 16   C. 30   D. 40

    1.____

2. Concrete for a self-supporting floor should have a slump, in inches, of about

    A. 3   B. 4   C. 7   D. 13

    2.____

3. When building material bears a distinguishing mark of the manufacturer, the inspector should

    A. ignore it
    B. ask the contractor to remove it
    C. check to see if the mark is approved by the Board
    D. ask the contractor to obtain the manufacturer's specifications

    3.____

4. The letters *A.S.T.M.* followed by letters and numbers refer to

    A. standard tests of materials
    B. paragraphs in state laws
    C. sections, text, and meaning of the Building Code
    D. the structural training manual

    4.____

5. A frame building with 2 x 4 studding has an interior partition with 2 x 6 studding. The MOST probable reason for the heavier studding is to provide

    A. heat insulation   B. sound insulation
    C. room for a soil stack   D. room for steam pipes

    5.____

6. Ties and chairs are used in construction involving

    A. plain concrete   B. reinforced concrete
    C. masonry   D. structural steel

    6.____

7. Painting of steel reinfarcing bars is

    A. *bad,* because it impairs bond
    B. *good,* because it prevents rust
    C. *bad,* because it increases costs
    D. *good,* because use of different colors permits ready identification of the various sizes

    7.____

8. An inspector picks up a brick, which has just been laid, to inspect the bedding. No mortar adhered to the brick so the furrowing of the mortar is shown clearly.
The inspector is MOST concerned with the

   A. depth of the furrow
   B. width of the furrow
   C. depth and width of the furrow
   D. fact that no mortar adhered to the brick

9. Acoustic tile would MOST likely be used in

   A. ceilings   B. floors   C. bathrooms   D. kitchens

10. To determine the story heights of a building, you should look at the

    A. plan view   B. elevation view
    C. architect's rendition   D. perspective view

11. Kalamein work is

    A. metal-sheathed wood
    B. a type of enameling
    C. woodwork using different colored woods to make a pattern
    D. used in ornamental plastering

12. The weight of all permanent construction in a building is known as _____ load.

    A. permanent   B. live   C. dead   D. design

13. A layer of plaster which is scratched both horizontally and vertically is known as a

    A. scratch coat   B. bond coat
    C. brown coat   D. plaster base

14. When steel is given two coats of paint, a different color is used for the second coat

    A. for a pleasing contrast
    B. to avoid monotony for the painter
    C. for chemical reasons
    D. to insure full coverage by the second coat

15. A certificate of occupancy is required for a new building

    A. if it is a Class A multiple dwelling
    B. if it is a multiple dwelling
    C. if it is a dwelling
    D. regardless of whether or not it is a dwelling

16. New multiple dwelling of non-fireproof construction

    A. is not allowed
    B. must be outside the fire limits
    C. must not exceed 75 feet in height
    D. must not occupy more than 70% of the lot area

17. In an elevation view, round reinforcing bars in a reinforced concrete floor would appear as   17._____

    A. circles
    B. lines
    C. either circles or line
    D. triangles

18. The columns of a building are spaced 21'0" in one direction and 28'0" in the other. The length of a diagonal of a bay is, in feet, MOST NEARLY   18._____

    A. 35.0   B. 35.1   C. 36.2   D. 34.9

19. The use of peaveys or cant hooks to handle creosoted lumber in wood construction is   19._____

    A. *bad,* because it may expose untreated wood
    B. *good,* because the laborer will not get splinters in his hands
    C. *bad,* because the lumber is damaged by rolling
    D. *good,* because it is an efficient method

20. The end of a joist resting on a masonry wall is USUALLY cut on a bevel to   20._____

    A. prevent damage to the wall if the joist should fall during a fire
    B. provide circulation of air around the enclosed portion of the joist
    C. provide a larger bearing area
    D. reduce the wall opening required by the joist

21. Oiling of steel reinforcing bars for concrete is   21._____

    A. *good,* because it prevents rust
    B. *good,* because it makes handling in the forms easier
    C. *bad,* because there is a chemical reaction with the concrete
    D. *bad,* because it prevents adhesion of the concrete

22. A load-bearing cavity wall consists of a four inch wythe and an eight inch wythe with a two inch air space.
    In normal construction, the wider wythe   22._____

    A. should be the outer face of the wall
    B. should be the inner face of the wall
    C. may be either inner or outer face
    D. wastes material as the two wythes should be of equal thickness

23. Metal ties used in cavity walls sometimes have a crimp which is located in the air space when the tie is in place in the wall.
    This crimp serves to   23._____

    A. strengthen the tie
    B. add to the elasticity of the tie
    C. prevent water from traveling across the tie
    D. center the tie between the wythes

Questions 24-25.

DIRECTIONS: Questions 24 and 25 refer to the following statement and sketch.

A specification reads: *Net cross-sectional area of a masonry unit shall be taken as the gross cross-sectional area minus the area of cores or cellular space.*

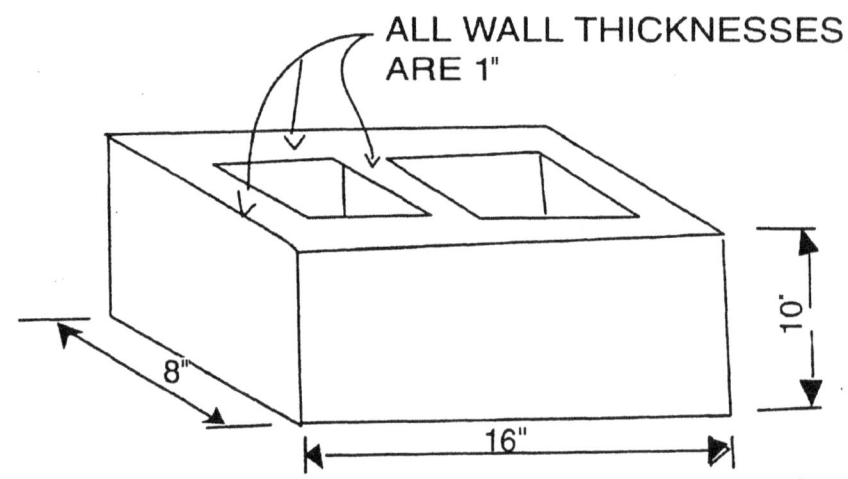

24. The gross cross-sectional area is _____ square inches.

    A. 64   B. 84   C. 128   D. 144

25. The net cross-sectional area is _____ square inches.

    A. 128   B. 112   C. 77   D. 50

26. Small wood members which are inserted in a diagonal position between floor joists for the purpose of bracing the joists and spreading loads to adjacent joists are called

    A. struts   B. ties   C. bridging   D. ledger strips

27. A beam placed perpendicular to joists and to which joists are nailed in framing for a chimney, stairway, or other opening, is called a

    A. trimmer joist B. tail beam
    C. girder   D. header

28. A narrow board let into the studding to provide added support for joists is known as a

    A. sill   B. trimmer   C. ribbon   D. sole plate

29. In concrete construction, honeycombing is MOST likely to occur in

    A. thin floors   B. thin walls
    C. heavy footing D. thick floors

30. The CHIEF objection to the use of green lumber in wood construction relates to its

    A. color
    B. strength
    C. lack of dimensional stability
    D. nailing

31. Concrete weighs 4000 pounds per cubic yard.
    A slab of concrete 4'3" wide by 7'6" long by 1'9" thick weighs, in pounds, MOST NEARLY

    A. 7550 B. 7950 C. 8000 D. 8260

32. A fire-resistive rating of an assembly is given in units of

    A. degrees centigrade
    B. degrees fahrenheit
    C. hours
    D. none of the above

33. A trimmer arch would be used in

    A. floor openings
    B. wall openings
    C. floor construction near chimneys
    D. parapet walls

34. Cracks in lumber due to contraction along annual rings are known as

    A. checks B. pitch pockets C. wane D. craze

35. The length of a tenpenny nail, in inches, is

    A. 2 1/2 B. 3 C. 3 1/2 D. 4

36. When ready-mix concrete is used on a job, the PRIMARY responsibility for checking the proportioning of cement, sand, and gravel rests with

    A. the inspector on the job
    B. the engineer on the job
    C. the inspector at the batching plant
    D. none of the above

37. In plastering, coves are

    A. never required
    B. used to obtain an even finish
    C. required where floor and wall meet
    D. sometimes required where wall and ceiling meet

38. Wood bridging should

    A. be nailed top and bottom before placing the subflooring
    B. not be placed until the subflooring is placed
    C. be nailed at its upper end only before the subflooring is placed
    D. be nailed at its lower end only before the subflooring is placed

39. Cross-furring is required by the Code in

    A. walls consisting of 2 x 4 studding
    B. ceilings when lath is attached directly to the wood joists of the floor above
    C. walls using metal lath on wood studs
    D. suspended ceilings

40. Board measure is a measure of

    A. length B. area C. volume D. weight

41. The consistency of concrete is measured by a _____ test.

    A. slump
    B. penetration
    C. strength
    D. time of set

42. Bricking up the space between furring at floors is done to

    A. provide corbelling
    B. fire-stop the wall
    C. stiffen the structure
    D. moisture-proof the wall

43. The dressed size of lumber is

    A. smaller than the nominal size
    B. depends upon the grade of the lumber
    C. its size as finally used on the job
    D. not related to its nominal size

44. Of the following types of joints, the one which is LEAST related to the others is

    A. raked B. weather C. construction D. struck

45. A rowlock course consists of bricks

    A. set on end
    B. set on their sides
    C. set flat
    D. laid alternately as headers and stretchers

46. With respect to flooring, shrinkage in a wood joist is MOST serious in

    A. length
    B. width
    C. depth
    D. all of the above

47. Neat cement and marble chips are used

    A. as mortar in marble walls and floors
    B. to make terrazzo
    C. for stucco
    D. for ornamental ceilings

48. Cinder concrete is sometimes used in floor construction in place of stone concrete because the cinder concrete

    A. permits thinner floors
    B. provides better acoustics
    C. is more fire-resistant
    D. is lighter

49. If a subcontractor's work is unsatisfactory,

    A. inform him that his payments will be withheld
    B. make the subcontractor's foreman rip it out
    C. so inform the general contractor
    D. warn him that further unsatisfactory work will bar him from future city work

50. *Extra work* is work
   A. not called for in the contract
   B. required to correct unsatisfactory work
   C. done outside of regular hours
   D. required by inexperienced inspectors which is unnecessary

50._____

KEY (CORRECT ANSWERS)

1. D	11. A	21. D	31. D	41. A
2. B	12. C	22. B	32. C	42. B
3. C	13. A	23. C	33. C	43. A
4. A	14. D	24. C	34. A	44. C
5. C	15. D	25. D	35. B	45. B
6. B	16. C	26. C	36. C	46. C
7. A	17. C	27. D	37. D	47. B
8. D	18. A	28. C	38. C	48. D
9. A	19. A	29. B	39. D	49. C
10. B	20. A	30. C	40. C	50. A

TEST 2

DIRECTIONS: Each question or incomplete statement is followed by several suggested answers or completions. Select the one that BEST answers the question or completes the statement. *PRINT THE LETTER OF THE CORRECT ANSWER IN THE SPACE AT THE RIGHT.*

1. Aggregates used to make concrete do NOT include

    A. sand B. gravel C. cement D. crushed rock

2. Careful slushing of the end joints of slip sills is PRIMARILY required to

    A. prevent displacement B. provide water tightness
    C. maintain bond D. prevent discoloration

3. The use of bats in brick work is justified when such use

    A. is required by the bond
    B. reduces the amount of face brick
    C. eliminates headers
    D. prevents waste of excess bats

4. In construction work, a neat line is a(n) _____ line.

    A. inside B. outside C. vertical D. center

5. In acceptable concrete practice, a small w/c ratio is MOST likely to indicate that the concrete mix will

    A. be stiff
    B. produce high-strength concrete
    C. have a big slump
    D. produce low-strength concrete

6. In concrete work, wooden form spreaders should be removed

    A. as soon as the concrete is placed
    B. after the concrete has attained initial set
    C. after the concrete has attained final set
    D. after the concrete has attained full strength

7. The rounded, projecting edge of a stair tread is the

    A. coping B. nosing C. rising D. stringing

8. A fire tower differs from fire stairs PRINCIPALLY in

    A. capacity
    B. location
    C. height
    D. tread and riser requirements

9. The area of a circle 2'6" in diameter is, in square feet, MOST NEARLY

    A. 4.6 B. 4.9 C. 5.3 D. 6.7

10. A cantilever beam would MOST likely be used in connection with a   10.____

    A. floor opening   B. balcony
    C. warehouse floor   D. roof opening

11. The Code requires various thicknesses of concrete cover for reinforcing rods used in the   11.____
    different elements of a building.
    That element which requires the LEAST cover is

    A. column   B. beam   C. girder   D. flat slab

12. A specification reads: *The span length of freely supported beams shall be the clear span*   12.____
    plus the effective depth of beam, but shall be within the distance between centers of sup-
    ports.
    According to this specification, the span length of such a beam with an effective depth
    of 22 inches, supported on 18 inch walls spaced 16'0" in the clear, is

    A. 17'9"   B. 17'7"   C. 17'6"   D. 17'5"

13. Bond plaster would be used   13.____

    A. where a fine, hard finish is required
    B. on concrete surfaces
    C. between scratch and finish coats
    D. on certain types of lath

14. A concealed draft opening is MOST closely associated with   14.____

    A. ventilation   B. heating
    C. fire-stopping   D. air conditioning

15. In estimating the cost of a reinforced concrete structure, the contractor would be LEAST   15.____
    concerned with

    A. volume of concrete
    B. surface area of forms
    C. pounds of reinforcing steel
    D. type of coarse aggregate

16. A brick wall is to be plastered.   16.____
    The BEST type of joint for this surface of the wall is

    A. flush   B. weathered   C. concave   D. raked

17. A groove is cut in the underside of a stone sill to   17.____

    A. keep water from the wall
    B. improve the bond with the wall
    C. conceal reinforcing
    D. reduce the weight of the sill

18. Joists spaced 16" o.c. on a 12'0" span support a floor which is to carry a live load of 80   18.____
    pounds per square foot. The TOTAL live load carried by a single joist is, in pounds,

    A. 590   B. 920   C. 1195   D. 1280

19. Pointing up around the end of a joist resting on a brick wall is

    A. *good*, because it improves appearance
    B. *bad*, because it may cause rotting of joist
    C. *good*, because it results in a more solid wall
    D. *bad*, because it interferes with fire-stopping

20. In a roof, the LONGEST rafters are _____ rafters.

    A. common
    B. hip jack
    C. valley jack
    D. either hip or valley jack

21. The thickness of lumber used for grounds is USUALLY, in inches,

    A. 7/32   B. 3/4   C. 25/32   D. 15/32

22. The terms *plank, scantling, heavy joists*, when used in connection with lumber, refer to

    A. dimensions   B. use   C. grade   D. finish

23. The Code provides that cold bends in reinforcing bars for concrete work shall have a radius at LEAST equal to the least dimension of the bar multiplied by

    A. 1   B. 2   C. 3   D. 4

24. According to the Code, gas cutting of structural steel is NOT permitted

    A. unless the member cut is carrying stress
    B. in preparation for welding
    C. to replace the milling of surfaces
    D. under any circumstances

25. In building construction, an apron would MOST likely be installed by a

    A. carpenter
    B. sheet-metal worker
    C. bricklayer
    D. glazier

26. In a building with masonry walls, furring

    A. is of no advantage
    B. is of no help in preventing wetting of plaster
    C. is used only because it provides a nailing surface
    D. adds to the insulating quality of the wall

27. Oil is applied to the inside surfaces of concrete forms PRIMARILY to

    A. make form removal easier
    B. provide a smoother finish to the concrete
    C. prevent leakage of water from the concrete
    D. neutralize acids present in the wood

28. A deformed reinforcing rod is superior to an equivalent smooth rod because it

    A. permits better bond with the concrete
    B. has greater tensile strength
    C. weighs more
    D. is easier to bend

29. In the usual six-story multiple dwelling, fire escapes are   29.____
    A. supported on floor joists cantilevered out through the walls
    B. supported on a framework tied to, but otherwise independent of, the building
    C. hung from the parapet
    D. supported on brackets which are bolted to channels on the innerside of the wall

30. A building on a lot 50'0" wide by 110'0" deep has a rectangular court 37'0" long by 8'6"   30.____
    wide.
    The area of the court is the following percentage of the area of the lot:
    A. 6.4   B. 6.2   C. 5.8   D. 5.7

KEY (CORRECT ANSWERS)

1.	C	16.	D
2.	B	17.	A
3.	A	18.	D
4.	B	19.	B
5.	B	20.	A
6.	A	21.	C
7.	B	22.	A
8.	B	23.	B
9.	B	24.	C
10.	B	25.	A
11.	D	26.	D
12.	C	27.	A
13.	B	28.	A
14.	C	29.	D
15.	D	30.	D

EXAMINATION SECTION
TEST 1

DIRECTIONS: Each question or incomplete statement is followed by several suggested answers or completions. Select the one that BEST answers the question or completes the statement. *PRINT THE LETTER OF THE CORRECT ANSWER IN THE SPACE AT THE RIGHT.*

Questions 1-5.

DIRECTIONS: For Questions 1 through 5, inclusive, Column I lists frequently used construction terms. Column II lists some of the building trades. For each item listed in Column I, enter in the appropriate space at the right the capital letter in front of the trade listed in Column II that is MOST closely associated with the item. Each trade may be used more than once or not at all.

COLUMN I	COLUMN II
1. Bed	A. Plumbing
2. Wiping	B. Plastering
3. Brown	C. Carpentry
4. Key	D. Masonry
5. Bridging	E. Painting
	F. Steelwork
	G. Roofing

1.____
2.____
3.____
4.____
5.____

6. A *cricket* would be found

    A. on a roof
    B. at a structural steel connection
    C. supporting reinforcing steel
    D. over a window

6.____

7. *Cutting in* is done when

    A. trimming a stud to size
    B. fitting a bat in a brick wall
    C. painting in tight corners
    D. trimming tallow for a wiped joint

7.____

8. *Corbeling* results in

    A. strengthening a concrete column
    B. waterproofing a foundation wall
    C. anchoring a steel girder to a bearing wall
    D. increasing the thickness of a brick wall

8.____

9. Solder used for copper gutters is MOST frequently

   A. 30-70 B. 40-60 C. 50-50 D. 60-40

10. A jack rafter runs from

    A. plate to ridge
    B. hip to ridge
    C. plate to hip
    D. plate to plate

11. The one of the following items that is LEAST related to the others is

    A. sill B. joist C. sole D. newel

12. A *fire cut* is made on

    A. timber posts
    B. rafters
    C. floor joists
    D. lathing

13. The one of the following items that is LEAST related to the others is

    A. joist hanger
    B. pintle
    C. bridle iron
    D. stirrup

14. The PROPER order of nailing sub-flooring and bridging is

    A. top of bridging, bottom of bridging, sub-flooring
    B. bottom of bridging, sub-flooring, top of bridging
    C. top of bridging, sub-flooring, bottom of bridging
    D. bottom of bridging, top of bridging, sub-flooring

15. Sleepers would be found in

    A. walls B. doors C. footings D. floors

16. The one of the following woods that is MOST commonly used for finish flooring is

    A. hemlock B. cypress C. larch D. oak

17. Spacing of studs in a stud partition is MOST frequently _____" o.c.

    A. 12 B. 14 C. 16 D. 18

18. A hollow masonry wall should be used in preference to a solid masonry wall when the characteristic MOST desired is

    A. insulation
    B. strength
    C. beauty
    D. durability

19. The arrangement of headers and stretchers in brickwork is known as the

    A. bond B. stringer C. lacing D. stile

20. Of the following, the reason that is LEAST likely to justify pointing brickwork is that pointing _____ the wall.

    A. improves the appearance of
    B. helps prevent cracking of
    C. increases the useful life of
    D. helps waterproof

21. The purpose of flashing is to   21.____

    A. keep water out   B. speed the set of mortar
    C. anchor a cornice   D. cover exposed joists

22. The one of the following classes of wall that would LEAST likely be the outside wall of a   22.____
    building is a

    A. spandrel   B. fire   C. curtain   D. parapet

23. Lime is added to mortar USUALLY to   23.____

    A. increase the strength of the mortar
    B. make the mortar water resistant
    C. make it easier to apply the mortar
    D. improve the appearance of the mortar joint

24. Efflorescence on the face of a brick wall is BEST removed by scrubbing with a solution of   24.____

    A. muriatic acid   B. sodium silicate
    C. oxalic acid   D. calcium oxide

25. The one of the following that is NOT a defect in painting is   25.____

    A. chalking   B. checking
    C. alligatoring   D. waning

26. The one of the following ingredients of a paint that would be called the *vehicle* is   26.____

    A. white lead   B. turpentine
    C. linseed oil   D. pigment

27. The one of the following that is used as a rust preventative in the prime coat for painting   27.____
    steel is

    A. aluminum   B. red lead
    C. titanium dioxide   D. carbon black

28. *Boxing*, with reference to paint, means   28.____

    A. thinning   B. mixing   C. spreading   D. drying

29. When painting new wood, filling of nail holes and cracks with putty should be done   29.____

    A. 24 hours before priming
    B. immediately before priming
    C. after priming and before the second coat
    D. after the second coat and before the finish coat

30. The one of the following that is the size of a reinforcing rod MOST commonly used in   30.____
    reinforced concrete construction is

    A. 1 3/4" ϕ B. 18 gauge   C. #9   D. 2 ST3

31. Honeycombing in concrete is USUALLY caused by   31.____

    A. too plastic a mix   B. high fall of concrete
    C. mixing too long   D. inadequate vibration

32. A concrete mix is indicated as 1:2:3 1/2 mix. The number 2 refers to the proportion by volume of

    A. water B. cement C. gravel D. sand

33. Specifications for concrete mixes frequently call for the use of dry sand. The reason for this is that the additional water in wet sand will

    A. make it more difficult to place the concrete
    B. decrease the strength of the concrete
    C. cause the sand and stone to segregate
    D. increase the cost of waterproofing

34. Curing of concrete serves PRIMARILY to

    A. prevent freezing of the concrete
    B. permit early removal of forms
    C. delay setting of the concrete
    D. prevent evaporation of moisture

35. The MAIN reason that forms for concrete work are oiled is to

    A. *permit* easy removal of forms
    B. *prevent* rust marks on the concrete
    C. *prevent* bleeding of water
    D. *permit* easier vibration of the concrete

36. The one of the following terms that is LEAST related to the others is

    A. 5-ply B. mastic
    C. vapor barrier D. flashing

37. Before quicklime can be used for plaster, it must be

    A. slaked B. burned C. floated D. glazed

38. When a hard plaster is required, as in halls, the one of the following that would MOST likely be used is

    A. lime B. Keene's cement
    C. stucco D. marbling

39. To give plaster a hard finish, hydrated lime is mixed with

    A. white cement B. linseed oil putty
    C. white lead D. plaster of paris

40. The purpose of a ground in plaster work is to

    A. provide a key for the plaster
    B. help the plasterer make an even wall
    C. prevent the plasterer's scaffold from slipping
    D. hold the loose plaster before it is placed

41. When a lightweight plaster is required, the one of the following fine aggregates that is MOST likely to be used is

    A. cinders
    B. sand
    C. talc
    D. vermiculite

42. Of the following fireproofing materials, the one which would be MOST frequently used to fireproof steel columns in a fireproof building is

    A. sheet rock
    B. vermiculite plaster
    C. brick
    D. rock lath

43. The one of the following items that is LEAST related to the others is

    A. rock wool
    B. wall board
    C. sheet rock
    D. rock lath

44. The first layer of plaster placed in a 3-coat plaster job is called the _____ coat.

    A. brown   B. scratch   C. hard   D. white

45. The one of the following symbols that represents a steel section which is MOST similar in appearance to a W section is

    A. U   B. L   C. I   D. Z

46. A plate used to connect two steel angles in a roof truss is known as a(n)

    A. angle iron
    B. gusset plate
    C. bearing plate
    D. tie bar

47. Steel beams are COMMONLY anchored to brick walls by

    A. government anchors
    B. tie rods
    C. eye bars
    D. anchor bolts

48. Rivet holes are lined up with a

    A. set screw
    B. ginnywink
    C. drift pin
    D. trivet

49. A sewer that carries BOTH storm water and sewage is called a _____ sewer.

    A. sanitary   B. flush   C. combined   D. mixed

50. A fresh air inlet for a house drainage system would be connected to the system

    A. just ahead of the house trap
    B. at each horizontal branch line
    C. at the top of the stack through the roof
    D. at the trap of each water closet

KEY (CORRECT ANSWERS)

1. D	11. D	21. A	31. D	41. D
2. A	12. C	22. B	32. D	42. B
3. B	13. B	23. C	33. B	43. A
4. B	14. C	24. A	34. D	44. B
5. C	15. D	25. D	35. A	45. C
6. A	16. D	26. C	36. C	46. B
7. C	17. C	27. B	37. A	47. A
8. D	18. A	28. B	38. B	48. C
9. C	19. A	29. C	39. D	49. C
10. C	20. B	30. C	40. B	50. A

TEST 2

DIRECTIONS: Each question or incomplete statement is followed by several suggested answers or completions. Select the one that BEST answers the question or completes the statement. *PRINT THE LETTER OF THE CORRECT ANSWER IN THE SPACE AT THE RIGHT.*

Questions 1-5.

DIRECTIONS: Column I consists of a list of trades, and Column II lists tools used in those trades. In the space at the right, opposite the number of the trade in Column I, write the letter preceding the tool of the trade in Column II.

COLUMN I	COLUMN II	
1. Carpenter	A. Mop	1.____
2. Plumber	B. Hawk	2.____
3. Plasterer	C. Miter box	3.____
4. Bricklayer	D. Shave-hook	4.____
5. Roofer	E. Jointing tool	5.____

Questions 6-7.

DIRECTIONS: Questions 6 and 7 refer to the mortar joints shown below.

6. The mortar joint MOST frequently used on common brickwork is   6.____
   A. 1 B. 2 C. 3 D. 4

7. The mortar joint which would NOT usually be made unless an outside scaffold was used is   7.____
   A. 1 B. 2 C. 3 D. 4

8. A rectangular yard is 50'0" long by 8'6" wide.   8.____
   The area of the yard is, in square feet,
   A. 420.0 B. 422.5 C. 425.0 D. 427.5

9. A rectangular court is 23'0" long by 9'6" wide.
   The length of the diagonal is MOST NEARLY

   A. 24'8"   B. 24'10"   C. 25'2"   D. 25'6"

10. Concrete weighs 150 pounds per cubic foot.
    A slab of concrete 6'0" long by 3'6" wide by 1'4" thick weighs MOST NEARLY _____ pounds.

    A. 4150   B. 4200   C. 4250   D. 4300

11. A building 32'0" by 65'0" occupies a lot 60'0" by 110'0". The ratio of building area to lot area is MOST NEARLY

    A. 0.32   B. 0.33   C. 0.34   D. 0.35

12. When painting wood, puttying of nail holes and cracks is done

    A. before any painting is started
    B. after the priming coat is applied
    C. after the finish coat is applied
    D. at any stage in the painting

13. The process of pouring paint from one container to another in order to mix it is known as

    A. bleeding   B. boxing   C. cutting   D. stirring

14. Paint is *thinned* with

    A. linseed oil   B. turpentine
    C. varnish   D. gasoline

15. A wood screw which can be tightened by a wrench is known as a _____ screw.

    A. lag   B. Philips   C. carriage   D. monkey

16. To permit easy removal of forms from concrete, the inside surfaces of the forms are often coated with

    A. paint   B. oil   C. water   D. asphalt

17. Sixteen pieces of 2 x 4 lumber, each 10'6" long, contain a total of _____ FBM.

    A. 110   B. 111   C. 112   D. 113

18. The consistency of concrete is measured with a

    A. Vicat needle   B. slump cone
    C. hook gage   D. bourdon gage

19. End-matched lumber would MOST likely be used for

    A. sheathing   B. roofing   C. flooring   D. siding

20. A post or shore is to be placed midway between columns to support the formwork for a reinforced concrete girder. The post should be cut

    A. short, so that wedging is required
    B. to exact length

C. long, so that it will have to be driven into place
D. in two pieces, to permit jackknifing into place

21. Batter boards are set by a

    A. mason   B. plumber   C. roofer   D. surveyor

22. Of the following terms, all of which refer to tools, the one which is LEAST related to the others is

    A. back   B. box-end   C. cross-cut   D. rip

23. Of the following tools, the one which is LEAST like the others is

    A. brace and bit   B. draw-knife
    C. plans   D. spoke-shave

24. When wood splits easily, it is advisable to drill a hole for each nail. The hole for the nail should be _____ the nail.

    A. larger in diameter than
    B. smaller in diameter than
    C. exactly the same diameter as
    D. less than one-quarter the length of

25. The length of a 10-penny nail, in inches, is

    A. $2\frac{1}{2}$ B. 3   C. $3\frac{1}{2}$ D. 4

26. The decimal equivalent of 31/64 of an inch is MOST NEARLY

    A. 0.45   B. 0.46   C. 0.47   D. 0.48

27. Of the following, the one which is BEST classified as an abrasive is

    A. a saw   B. a chisel   C. graphite   D. sandpaper

28. Of the following construction materials, the one which would MOST likely be stored directly on the ground is

    A. brick   B. cement   C. steel   D. wood

29. The strength of brick walls is based upon the type of mortar used.
    The relative strength of the various types of mortar, in descending order, is

    A. cement, lime, cement-lime
    B. lime, cement-lime, cement
    C. cement-lime, cement, lime
    D. cement, cement-lime, lime

30. Coating reinforcing rods with oil before placing them in the forms is

    A. *good* practice, because it prevents rusting
    B. *poor* practice, because it makes the rods difficult to handle
    C. *good* practice if the forms are oiled
    D. *poor* practice, because it destroys the bond between the concrete and the rods

31. If the mixing plant should break down after one-half the concrete has been mixed for a floor, the BEST thing to do would be to

    A. take the concrete out of the forms and throw it away
    B. spread the available concrete evenly over the floor area
    C. block off one-half of the floor area and place the available concrete in the blocked-off area
    D. keep mixing the concrete in the forms with shovels until the plant is repaired

32. Splicing of reinforcing bars is accomplished by

    A. using wire ties
    B. underlapping the bars
    C. hooking the bars
    D. using metal clips

33. A sanitary sewer carries

    A. storm water only
    B. sewage only
    C. sewage and storm water
    D. the discharge from a sewage plant

34. A neat line

    A. is the result of good workmanship
    B. is used in concrete construction only
    C. defines an outer limit of a structure
    D. defines an outer limit of excavation for a structure

35. Continued trowelling of a cement-finish floor for a building is

    A. *good* practice, because it provides a smooth floor
    B. *poor* practice, because it produces a slippery floor
    C. *poor* practice, because it brings the fines to the surface
    D. *good* practice, because it insures proper mixing of the cement finish

36. In reinforced concrete form work, a beveled chamfer strip is used to

    A. reinforce the outside of the forms
    B. reinforce the inside of the forms
    C. seal leaks in the forms
    D. do none of the foregoing

37. Cracks in lumber due to contraction along annual rings are known as

    A. checks
    B. wanes
    C. pitch pockets
    D. dry rot

38. Honeycombing is MOST likely to occur in construction involving

    A. steel   B. concrete   C. wood   D. masonry

39. Floor beams are sometimes crowned to

    A. provide arch action
    B. eliminate deflection
    C. strengthen the floor
    D. provide a more nearly level floor than would be provided by straight beams

40. In brickwork, a rowlock course consists of   40.____

   A. headers
   B. stretchers
   C. bricks laid on edge
   D. bricks laid so that the longest dimension is vertical

41. The term *bond,* as used in bricklaying, refers to   41.____

   A. structure only
   B. pattern only
   C. structure and pattern
   D. color and finish of individual bricks

42. Concrete is a mixture of cement,   42.____

   A. fine aggregate, coarse aggregate, and water
   B. sand, and water
   C. stone, and water
   D. sand, and stone

43. Consistency, when used in connection with concrete, refers to the   43.____

   A. seven-day strength
   B. twenty-eight day strength
   C. initial set before forms are removed
   D. plasticity of freshly mixed concrete

44. Brick may be used for the facing material in both faced walls and veneered walls. The distinction between the two types of walls relates to   44.____

   A. bonding or lack of bonding between facing and backing
   B. type of material in facing and backing
   C. relative thickness of facing and backing
   D. the type of mortar used

45. A plaster *key* is NOT formed on _____ lath.   45.____

   A. wood   B. metal
   C. expanded metal   D. gypsum

46. Of the following, the BEST tool to use to make a hole in a coping stone is a   46.____

   A. star drill   B. coping saw
   C. pneumatic grinder   D. diamond wheel dresser

47. Roughing refers to work performed by a   47.____

   A. carpenter   B. bricklayer
   C. plumber   D. roofer

48. A post supporting a handrail is known as a   48.____

   A. tread   B. riser   C. newel   D. bevel

49. The live load on a floor is 40 pounds per square foot. The floor joists are on a 14'0" span and are spaced 2'6" on centers.
    The maximum live load carried by a joist, in pounds, is MOST NEARLY

    A. 700   B. 933   C. 1167   D. 1400

50. Of the following terms, the one LEAST related to the others is

    A. ground
    C. rafter
    B. purlin
    D. ridge board

KEY (CORRECT ANSWERS)

1. C	11. A	21. D	31. C	41. C
2. D	12. B	22. B	32. A	42. A
3. B	13. B	23. A	33. B	43. D
4. E	14. B	24. B	34. C	44. A
5. A	15. A	25. B	35. C	45. D
6. C	16. B	26. D	36. D	46. A
7. A	17. C	27. D	37. A	47. C
8. C	18. B	28. A	38. B	48. C
9. B	19. C	29. D	39. D	49. D
10. B	20. A	30. D	40. C	50. A

EXAMINATION SECTION
TEST 1

DIRECTIONS: Each question or incomplete statement is followed by several suggested answers or completions. Select the one that BEST answers the question or completes the statement. *PRINT THE LETTER OF THE CORRECT ANSWER IN THE SPACE AT THE RIGHT.*

1. The combustion efficiency of a boiler can be determined with a CO_2 indicator and the   1._____

    A. under fire draft
    B. boiler room humidity
    C. flue gas temperature
    D. outside air temperature

2. A quick, practical method of determining if the cast-iron waste pipe delivered to a job has been damaged in transit is to   2._____

    A. hydraulically test it
    B. "ring" each length with a hammer
    C. drop each length to see whether it breaks
    D. visually examine the pipe for cracks

3. An electrostatic precipitator is used to   3._____

    A. filter the air supply
    B. remove sludge from the fuel oil
    C. remove particles from the fuel gas
    D. supply samples for an Orsat analysis

4. The PRIMARY cause of cracking and spalling of refractory lining in the furnace of a steam generator is *most likely* due to   4._____

    A. continuous over-firing of boiler
    B. slag accumulation on furnace walls
    C. change in fuel from solid to liquid
    D. uneven heating and cooling within the refractory brick

5. The term "effective temperature" in air conditioning means   5._____

    A. the dry bulb temperature
    B. the average of the wet and dry bulb temperatures
    C. the square root of the product of wet and dry bulb temperatures
    D. an arbitrary index combining the effects of temperature, humidity, and movement

6. The piping in all buildings having dual water distribution systems should be identified by a color coding of _____ for potable water lines and _____ for non-potable water lines.   6._____

    A. green; red
    B. green; yellow
    C. yellow; green
    D. yellow; red

7. The breaking of a component of a machine subjected to excessive vibration is called   7._____

    A. tensile failure
    B. fatigue failure
    C. caustic embrittlement
    D. amplitude failure

8. The TWO MOST important factors to be considered in selecting fans for ventilating systems are

    A. noise and efficiency
    B. space available and weight
    C. first cost and dimensional bulk
    D. construction and arrangement of drive

9. In the modern power plant deaerator, air is removed from water to

    A. reduce heat losses in the heaters
    B. reduce corrosion of boiler steel due to the air
    C. reduce the load of the main condenser air pumps
    D. prevent pumps from becoming vapor bound

10. The abbreviations BOD, COD, and DO are associated with

    A. flue gas analysis   B. air pollution control
    C. boiler water treatment   D. water pollution control

11. The piping of a newly installed drainage system should be tested upon completion of the rough plumbing with a head of water of NOT LESS THAN _____ feet.

    A. 10   B. 15   C. 20   D. 25

12. Of the following statements concerning aquastats, the one which is CORRECT is:

    A. Aquastats may be obtained with either a narrow or wide range of settings
    B. Aquastats have a mercury tube switch which is controlled by the stack switch
    C. An aquastat is a device used to shut down the burner in the event of low water in the boiler
    D. An aquastat should be located about 4 inches above the normal water line of the boiler

13. The SAFEST way to protect the domestic water supply from contamination by sewage or non-potable water is to insert

    A. air gaps
    B. swing connections
    C. double check valves
    D. tanks with overhead discharge

14. The MAIN function of a back-pressure valve which is sometimes found in the connection between a water drain pipe and the sewer system is to

    A. equalize the pressure between the drain pipe and the sewer
    B. prevent sewer water from flowing into the drain pipe
    C. provide pressure to enable waste to reach the sewer
    D. make sure that there is not too much water pressure in the sewer line

15. Boiler water is neutral if its pH value is

    A. 0   B. 1   C. 7   D. 14

16. A domestic hot water mixing or tempering valve should be preceded in the hot water line by a

    A. strainer
    B. foot valve
    C. check valve
    D. steam trap

17. Between a steam boiler and its safety valve there should be

    A. no valve of any type
    B. a gate valve of the same size as the safety valve
    C. a swing check valve of at least the same size as the safety valve
    D. a cock having a clear opening equal in area to the pipe connecting the boiler and safety valve

18. A diagram of horizontal plumbing drainage lines should have cleanouts shown

    A. at least every 25 feet
    B. at least every 100 feet
    C. wherever a basin is located
    D. wherever a change in direction occurs

19. When a Bourdon gauge is used to measure steam pressures, some form of siphon or water seal must be maintained.
    The reason for this is to

    A. obtain "absolute" pressure readings
    B. prevent steam from entering the gage
    C. prevent condensate from entering the gage
    D. obtain readings below atmospheric pressure

20. In a closed heat exchanger, oil is cooled by condensate which is to be returned to a boiler. In order to avoid the possibility of contaminating the condensate with oil should a tube fail in the oil cooler, it would be good practice to

    A. cool the oil by air instead of water
    B. treat the condensate with an oil solvent
    C. keep the oil pressure in the exchanger higher than the water pressure
    D. keep the water pressure in the exchanger higher than the oil pressure

21. A radiator thermostatic trap is used on a vacuum return type of heating system to

    A. release the pocketed air only
    B. reduce the amount of condensate
    C. maintain a predetermined radiator water level
    D. prevent the return of live steam to the return line

22. According to the color coding of piping, fire protection piping should be painted

    A. green   B. yellow   C. purple   D. red

23. The MAIN purpose of a standpipe system is to

    A. supply the roof water tank
    B. provide water for firefighting

C. circulate water for the heating system
D. provide adequate pressure for the water supply

24. The name "Saybolt" is associated with the measurement of

   A. viscosity
   B. Btu content
   C. octane rating
   D. temperature

25. Recirculation of conditioned air in an air-conditioned building is done MAINLY to

   A. reduce refrigeration tonnage required
   B. increase room entrophy
   C. increase air specific humidity
   D. reduce room temperature below the dewpoint

26. In a plumbing installation, vent pipes are GENERALLY used to

   A. prevent the loss of water seal from traps by evaporation
   B. prevent the loss of water seal due to several causes other than evaporation
   C. act as an additional path for liquids to flow through during normal use of a plumbing fixture
   D. prevent the backflow of water in a cross-connection between a drinking water line and a sewage line

27. The designation "150 W" cast on the bonnet of a gate valve is an indication of the

   A. water working temperature
   B. water working pressure
   C. area of the opening in square inches
   D. weight of the valve in pounds

28. In the city, the size soil pipe necessary in a sewage drainage system is determined by the

   A. legal occupancy of the building
   B. vertical height of the soil line
   C. number of restrooms connected to the soil line
   D. number of "fixture units" connected to the soil line

29. Fins or other extended surfaces are used on heat exchanger tubes when

   A. the exchanger is a water-to-water exchanger
   B. water is on one side of the tube and condensing steam on the other side
   C. the surface coefficient of heat transfer on both sides of the tube is high
   D. the surface coefficient of heat transfer on one side of the tube is low compared to the coefficient on the other side of the tube

30. A fusible plug may be put in a fire tube boiler as an emergency device to indicate low water level. The fusible plug is installed so that under normal operating conditions,

   A. both sides are exposed to steam
   B. one side is exposed to water and the other side to steam
   C. one side is exposed to steam and the other side to hot gases
   D. one side is exposed to the water and the other side to hot gases

31. Extra strong wrought-iron pipe, as compared to standard wrought-iron pipe of the same nominal size, has

    A. the same outside diameter but a smaller inside diameter
    B. the same inside diameter but a larger outside diameter
    C. a larger outside diameter and a smaller inside diameter
    D. larger inside and outside diameters

32. Fans may be rated on a dynamic or a static efficiency basis. The dynamic efficiency would *probably* be

    A. lower in value because of the energy absorbed by the air velocity
    B. the same as the static in the case of centrifugal blowers running at various speeds
    C. the same as the static in the case of axial flow blowers running at various speeds
    D. higher in value than the static

33. The function of the stack relay in an oil burner installation is to

    A. regulate the draft over the fire
    B. regulate the flow of fuel oil to the burner
    C. stop the motor if the oil has not ignited
    D. stop the motor if the water or steam pressure is too high

34. The type of centrifugal pump which is inherently balanced for hydraulic thrust is the

    A. double suction impeller type
    B. single suction impeller type
    C. single stage type
    D. multistage type

35. The specifications for a job using sheet lead calls for "4-lb. sheet lead." This means that each sheet should weigh

    A. 4 lbs.
    B. 4 lbs. per square
    C. 4 lbs. per square foot
    D. 4 lbs. per cubic inch

36. The total cooling load design conditions for a building are divided for convenience into two components.
    These are:

    A. infiltration and radiation
    B. sensible heat and latent heat
    C. wet and dry bulb temperatures
    D. solar heat gain and moisture transfer

37. The function of a Hartford loop used on some steam boilers is to

    A. limit boiler steam pressure
    B. limit temperature of the steam
    C. prevent high water levels in the boiler
    D. prevent back flow of water from the boiler into the return main

38. Vibration from a ventilating blower can be prevented from being transmitted to the duct work by

   A. installing straighteners in the duct
   B. throttling the air supply to the blower
   C. bolting the blower tightly to the duct
   D. installing a canvas sleeve at the blower outlet

38.____

39. A specification states that access panels to suspended ceiling will be of metal. The MAIN reason for providing access panels is to

   A. improve the insulation of the ceiling
   B. improve the appearance of the ceiling
   C. make it easier to construct the building
   D. make it easier to maintain the building

39.____

40. A plumber on a job reports that the steamfitter has installed a 3" steam line in a location at which the plans show the house trap. On inspecting the job, you should

   A. tell the steamfitter to remove the steam line
   B. study the condition to see if the house trap can be relocated
   C. tell the plumber and steamfitter to work it out between themselves and then report to you
   D. tell the plumber to find another location for the trap because the steamfitter has already completed his work

40.____

41. In the installation of any heating system, the MOST important consideration is that

   A. all elements be made of a good grade of cast iron
   B. all radiators and connectors be mounted horizontally
   C. the smallest velocity of flow of heating medium be used
   D. there be proper clearance between hot surfaces and surrounding combustible material

41.____

42. Which one of the following is the PRIMARY object in drawing up a set of specifications for materials to be purchased?

   A. Control of quality
   B. Outline of intended use
   C. Establishment of standard sizes
   D. Location and method of inspection.

42.____

43. The drawing which should be used as a LEGAL reference when checking completed construction work is the _____ drawing.

   A. contract
   B. assembly
   C. working or shop
   D. preliminary

43.____

Questions 44-50.

DIRECTIONS: Questions 44 through 50 refer to the plumbing drawing shown below.

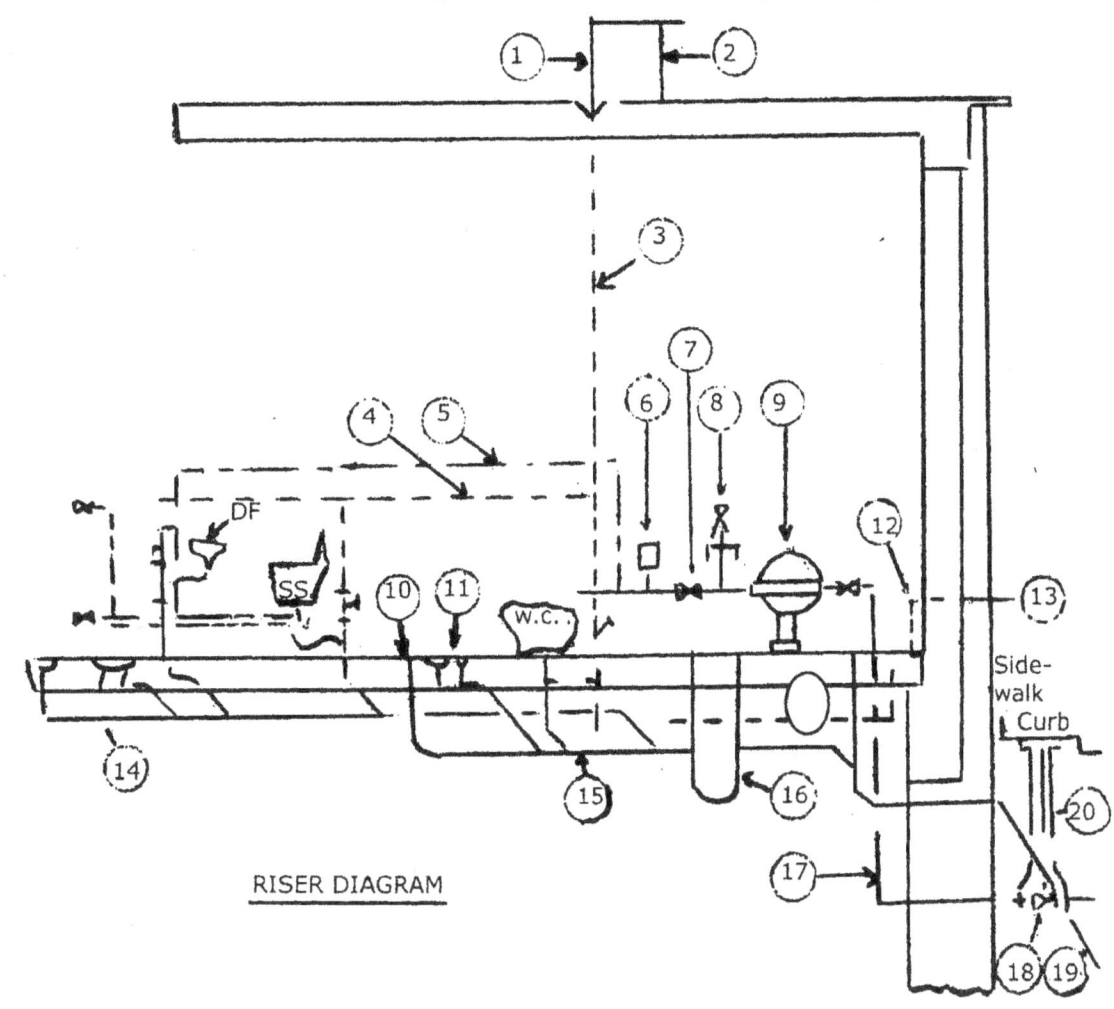

RISER DIAGRAM

44. According to the building code, the MINIMUM diameter of No. 1 and its minimum height, No. 2 respectively, are

    A. 2" and 12"   B. 3" and 18"
    C. 4" and 24"   D. 6" and 36"

44.____

45. No. 6 is a

    A. relief valve   B. shock absorber
    C. testing connection   D. drain

45.____

46. No. 9 is a

    A. strainer   B. float valve
    C. meter   D. pedestal

46.____

47. No. 11 is a

    A. floor drain   B. cleanout
    C. trap   D. vent connection

47.____

48. No. ⑬ is a

    A. standpipe   B. air inlet
    C. sprinkler head   D. cleanout

49. The size of No. ⑯ is

    A. 2" x 2"   B. 2" x 3"
    C. 3" x 3"   D. 4" x 4"

50. No. ⑱ is a

    A. pressure reducing valve
    B. butterfly valve
    C. curb cock
    D. sprinkler head

KEY (CORRECT ANSWERS)

1. C	11. A	21. D	31. A	41. D
2. B	12. C	22. D	32. D	42. A
3. C	13. A	23. B	33. C	43. A
4. D	14. B	24. A	34. A	44. C
5. D	15. C	25. A	35. C	45. B
6. B	16. A	26. B	36. B	46. C
7. B	17. A	27. B	37. D	47. A
8. A	18. D	28. D	38. D	48. B
9. B	19. B	29. D	39. D	49. D
10. D	20. D	30. D	40. B	50. C

EXAMINATION SECTION
TEST 1

DIRECTIONS: Each question or incomplete statement is followed by several suggested answers or completions. Select the one that BEST answers the question or completes the statement. *PRINT THE LETTER OF THE CORRECT ANSWER IN THE SPACE AT THE RIGHT.*

1. The dial of a water meter shall be a MAXIMUM height above the floor of _____ ft. 1._____

    A. 1 B. 2 C. 3 D. 4

2. A stop-and-waste cock is GENERALLY used on 2._____

    A. soil lines
    B. gas supply lines
    C. water supply lines subjected to low temperatures
    D. refrigerant lines connected to compressors

3. Assume that your superior has directed you to make certain changes in your established inspection procedure. After using this modified procedure on several inspections, you find that the original procedure was distinctly superior and you wish to return to it.
   You should 3._____

    A. let your superior find this out for himself
    B. simply change back to the original procedure
    C. compile definite data and information to prove your case to your superior
    D. persuade one of the more experienced inspectors to take this matter up with your superior

4. When automatic sprinklers are attached to a piping system containing air under pressure, the sprinkler system is called a _____ system. 4._____

    A. wet-pipe   B. dry-pipe
    C. deluge   D. compressed air

5. When making an inspection of one of the buildings under your supervision, the BEST procedure to follow in making a record of the inspection is to 5._____

    A. return immediately to the office and write a report from memory
    B. write down all the important facts during or as soon as you complete the inspection
    C. fix in your mind all important facts so that you can repeat them from memory if necessary
    D. fix in your mind all important facts so that you can make out your report at the end of the day

6. The MAIN reason for pitching a steam pipe in a heating system is to 6._____

    A. reduce friction in the pipe
    B. prevent the formation of scale
    C. facilitate repairs
    D. prevent accumulation of condensate

7. Nozzles on 2 1/2" diameter hose for standpipe systems must GENERALLY have a minimum length of _____ inches.

   A. 3 B. 6 C. 10 D. 15

8. An inspector visited a large building under construction. He inspected the soil lines at 9 M., water lines at 10 A.M., fixtures at 11 A.M., and did his office work in the afternoon. He followed the same pattern daily for weeks.
   This procedure was

   A. *good*, because it was methodical and he did not miss anything
   B. *good*, because it gave equal time to all phases of the plumbing
   C. *bad*, because not enough time was devoted to fixtures
   D. *bad*, because the tradesmen knew when the inspection would occur

9. When an unusually long run of supply pipe for sprinklers is needed, an increase in pipe size over that called for in the schedules may be required to

   A. compensate for increased friction
   B. provide enough water if the pipe diameter decreases due to corrosion deposits
   C. adequately protect areas which are separated by fire walls
   D. provide enough water in case more than one fire occurs at the same time

10. Roof drainage downspouts or leaders should be sized according to the

    A. type of sewer connection
    B. type of building occupancy
    C. size of cold water risers
    D. area of the roof to be drained

11. The type of pipe which is GENERALLY advantageous to use where corrosion is severe is

    A. cast iron   B. wrought iron
    C. steel   D. galvanized iron

12. A contractor has made an unjustified complaint against an inspector to the inspector's superior.
    In future contacts with this contractor, the inspector should be

    A. very careful in what he says
    B. courteous and fair in enforcing the law
    C. cool and distant to avoid more trouble
    D. exceptionally friendly in order to ease matters

13. A tank is filled with fresh water to a height of 20 ft. The pressure at the bottom of the tank is _____ pounds per square foot.

    A. 1168 B. 1248 C. 1322 D. 1404

14. The one of the following terms which is NOT used to classify buildings for purposes of sprinkler installations is _____ hazard.

    A. light B. ordinary C. regular D. extra

15. The PROPER type of fitting to use in a horizontal hot water heating main, when changing pipe size, is a(n)   15.____

    A. concentric reducer   B. eccentric reducer
    C. hexagon bushing   D. face bushing

16. Fire pumps shall be tested after installation to ascertain that the pump is supplying its rated capacity at   16.____

    A. the lowest required hose outlet
    B. the highest required hose outlet
    C. every hose outlet in the building
    D. one hose outlet which has been selected for testing

17. A pipe chase is a   17.____

    A. wire brush for cleaning the inside of pipes
    B. wire brush used for cleaning the outside of pipes
    C. continuous space in a building through which pipes run
    D. thimble through a wall to allow a pipe to pierce the wall

18. The utility line that USUALLY enters or leaves the building at the lowest elevation is the   18.____

    A. water inlet   B. gas line
    C. electric supply   D. building drain

19. The standpipe system shall be zoned by use of gravity tanks, automatic fire pumps, pressure tanks, and street pressure so that the MAXIMUM pressure at the inlet of any hose valve in the zone is _____ psig.   19.____

    A. 40   B. 60   C. 80   D. 100

20. Yard hydrant systems which are connected to city water mains shall be provided with post indicator valves located in an accessible position.
    Such post indicator valves shall be locked _____ and painted _____ .   20.____

    A. shut; green   B. shut; red
    C. open; green   D. open; red

21. A practice which is likely to cause some confusion when dealing with contractors is for an inspector to   21.____

    A. issue detailed instruction only in writing
    B. relay instructions to the contractor through one or two of the contractor's men
    C. transmit simple instructions orally
    D. follow up all his instructions after issuing them

22. Small commercial sizes of steel pipe are GENERALLY designated by their _____ diameter.   22.____

    A. exact inside   B. exact outside
    C. nominal inside   D. nominal outside

23. A head of water of 50 feet is equivalent to a pressure of MOST NEARLY _____ psi.   23.____

    A. 16   B. 22   C. 28   D. 34

24. A contractor demands to see your supervisor after accusing you of being prejudiced against him.
    The BEST course of action for you to follow is to

    A. convince him that you are not prejudiced
    B. remind him that you can make trouble for him if he fails to show you proper respect
    C. take him to your superior as he requests
    D. do nothing if you feel that you are not prejudiced

25. The water supply pipe which extends from the street main to the house control valve is GENERALLY called the _____ pipe.

    A. main   B. intake   C. service   D. gooseneck

26. The number of threads per inch on standard steel pipe threads GENERALLY

    A. decreases as the diameter of the pipe increases
    B. increases as the diameter of the pipe increases
    C. does not vary with the diameter of the pipe
    D. depends solely on the pressure the pipe must withstand

27. A specification requires that sewer pipe be laid with a smooth and uniform invert.
    The term *invert* refers to the _____ of the pipe, _____.

    A. inside; all around   B. outside; all around
    C. inside; at the bottom   D. outside; at the bottom

Questions 28-40.

DIRECTIONS: Questions 28 through 40 refer to the Riser Diagram shown below.

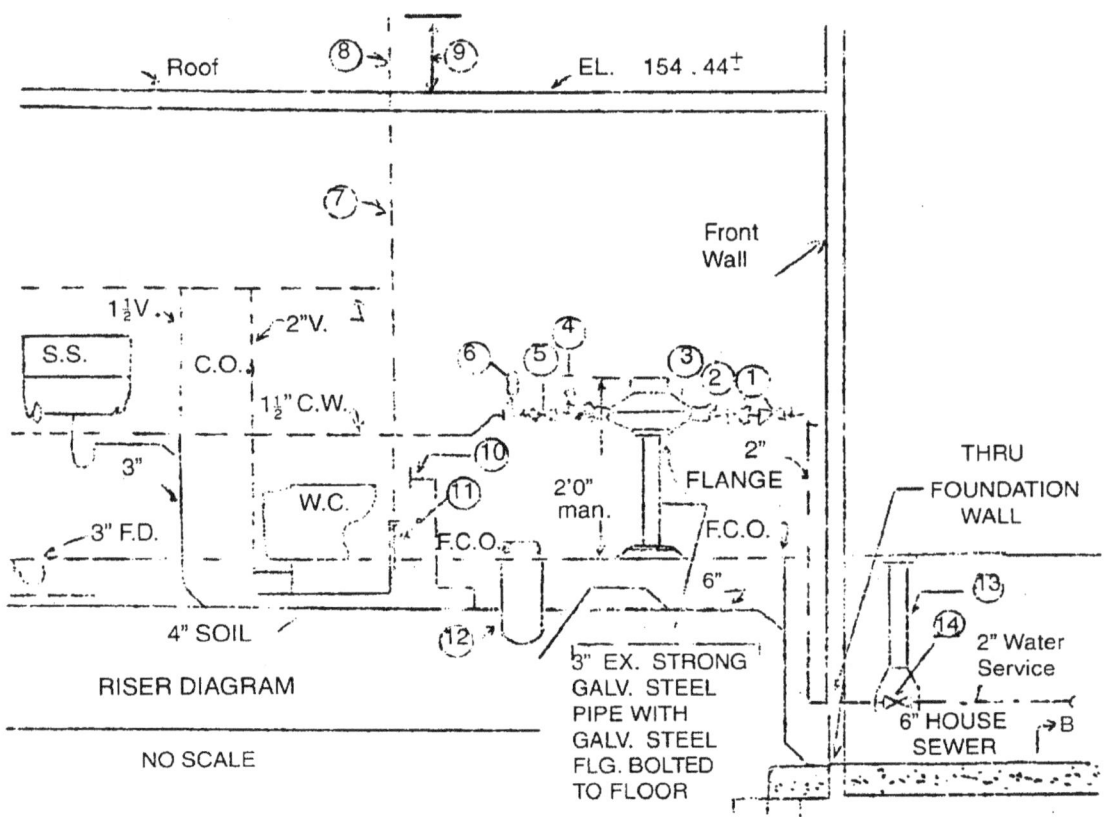

28. Item *1* is a _____ valve. 28._____
   A. check   B. globe   C. gate   D. pressure

29. Item *2* is a 29._____
   A. valve   B. union   C. reducer   D. flange

30. Item *3* is a 30._____
   A. meter
   C. water fountain
   B. sink
   D. reducing valve

31. Item *4* is a 31._____
   A. pressure valve
   C. relief fitting
   B. test connection
   D. supply valve

32. Item *6* is 32._____
   A. meter
   C. water indicator
   B. pressure gauge
   D. shock absorber

33. Item *7* is a 33._____
   A. soil line
   C. water supply line
   B. vent line
   D. heater exhaust

34. Item *8* should have a minimum diameter of _____ inches. 34._____
   A. 2   B. 3   C. 4   D. 6

35. Distance *9* should be a minimum of _____ ft. 35._____
   A. 1   B. 2   C. 4   D. 6

36. Item *10* is a 36._____
   A. sprinkler connection
   C. fresh air inlet
   B. clean-out plug
   D. floor drain

37. Item *11* is a 37._____
   A. hot water connection
   C. flushometer fitting
   B. clean-out plug
   D. floor drain

38. Item *12* is a 38._____
   A. trap
   C. floor drain
   B. running trap
   D. return bend

39. Item *13* is a 39._____
   A. curb box
   C. metering point
   B. sewer access
   D. pressure gage location

40. Item *14* has the main purpose of

    A. permitting water supply to be turned off
    B. reducing water supply pressure
    C. checking backflow
    D. permitting a pressure check

KEY (CORRECT ANSWERS)

1. C	11. A	21. B	31. B
2. C	12. B	22. C	32. D
3. C	13. B	23. B	33. B
4. B	14. C	24. C	34. C
5. B	15. B	25. C	35. B
6. D	16. B	26. A	36. C
7. D	17. C	27. C	37. B
8. D	18. D	28. C	38. B
9. A	19. B	29. C	39. A
10. D	20. D	30. A	40. A

TEST 2

DIRECTIONS: Each question or incomplete statement is followed by several suggested answers or completions. Select the one that BEST answers the question or completes the statement. *PRINT THE LETTER OF THE CORRECT ANSWER IN THE SPACE AT THE RIGHT.*

1. Two full lengths of black standard steel gas pipe in a continuous run should be connected together by a

    A. running thread coupling
    B. right and left coupling
    C. gasketed union
    D. tee with side outlet plugged

    1.____

2. The factor which is NOT generally considered to be a major cause of accidents is

    A. failure to use personal protective devices
    B. working at a very rapid speed
    C. using inoperative safety devices
    D. lack of familiarity with a particular job

    2.____

3. Underground mains and lead-in connections to system risers shall be flushed thoroughly before any connection is made to sprinkler piping in order to

    A. make sure that there are no leaks in the mains
    B. check that the pressure meets building code requirements
    C. make sure that the proper number of gpm can flow through the pipes
    D. remove foreign materials which may have entered during the course of installation

    3.____

4. A plumbing specification states: *Each pipe shall have clearly impressed on its outer surface the name of the manufacturer and of the factory in which it was made.* The BEST reason for this requirement is that this

    A. identifies the grade of the pipe
    B. helps locate the pipe in the field
    C. insures that approved material is used
    D. shows who is responsible for defective material

    4.____

5. A plumbing system should be tested at a water pressure which is determined by multiplying the working pressure of the system by a factor of

    A. 1.0   B. 1.25   C. 1.5   D. 2.0

    5.____

6. A *by-pass loop* in a piping system

    A. tends to eliminate pulsations of fluid flow
    B. provides a method for increasing the capacity of the piping system
    C. prevents excessive piping stresses by providing for expansion and contraction
    D. provides emergency routing of flow if the primary system is shut down

    6.____

7. In an accident report, the information which may be MOST useful in decreasing the recurrence of similar type accidents is the

   A. time the accident happened
   B. cause of the accident
   C. extent of injuries sustained
   D. number of people involved

8. Joints in glass pipe used for chemical waste should NOT be made by use of

   A. compression couplings   B. adapter couplings
   C. caulking   D. adjustable joints

9. Assume that 90 gallons per minute flow through a certain 3-inch pipe which is tapped into a street main.
   The amount of water which would flow through a 1-inch pipe tapped into the same street main is MOST NEARLY _____ gpm

   A. 90   B. 45   C. 30   D. 10

10. Accessible cleanouts in drainage piping shall be installed at each change of direction GREATER than _____ °.

    A. 20   B. 45   C. 90   D. 135

11. The kitchen sink in a dwelling may be used to receive the discharge of an indirect waste pipe from a

    A. clothes washer   B. dishwasher
    C. refrigerator   D. drinking fountain

12. The material which should NOT generally be used for roof drains is

    A. wrought iron   B. lead
    C. stainless steel   D. copper

13. The time required to pump 2500 gallons of water out of a sump at the rate of 12 1/2 gallons per minute would be _____ hour(s), _____ minutes.

    A. 1; 40   B. 2; 30   C. 3; 20   D. 6; 40

14. Copper tubing which has an inside diameter of 1 1/16 inches and a wall thickness of .095 inches has an outside diameter which is MOST NEARLY _____ inches.

    A. 1 5/32   B. 1 3/16   C. 1 7/32   D. 1 1/4

15. Valves used to control a standpipe system shall have the name of the manufacturer

    A. on a tag which is permanently attached to each valve by means of a chain
    B. cast on or in each valve
    C. on a tag which is welded to each valve
    D. readily available in the records kept by the building custodian

16. The PREFERRED type of feed to sprinklers, especially where there are over six sprinklers on a branch line is _____ feed.

    A. center central   B. central end
    C. side end   D. cross main

17. A *branch interval* is defined as

    A. the length along the center line of pipe and fittings both horizontal and vertical
    B. a distance along a soil or waste stack corresponding in general to a story height, but in no case less than 8 feet, within which the horizontal branches from one floor or story of a building are connected to the stack
    C. a vent connecting one or more individual vents with a vent stack or stack vent
    D. that part of a piping system other than a main riser or stack that extends to fixtures on two or less consecutive floors

18. The distance which is measured along the center line of pipes and fittings is called the _____ length.

    A. system
    B. effective
    C. equivalent
    D. developed

19. The HEAVIEST commercially obtainable steel and wrought iron pipe is called

    A. extra strong
    B. double extra strong
    C. heavy duty
    D. high strength

20. Pressure tanks for sprinkler systems should be located

    A. in the basement of the building
    B. at or above the top level of sprinklers
    C. at any convenient location in the building
    D. on any floor where they will be easily accessible

21. Fire pumps in standpipe systems should be

    A. in sump pits below the pump room floor level
    B. mounted directly on the pump room floor
    C. on concrete foundations at least 1 foot above the pump room floor level
    D. on concrete platforms at least 3 feet above the pump room floor level

22. A *street ell* is a fitting which has

    A. threads on the inside of one end and on the outside of the other end
    B. threads on the inside of both ends
    C. threads on the outside of both ends
    D. non-tapered threads on both ends

23. The MAIN difference between schedule-80 pipe and schedule-40 pipe is that schedule-80 pipe

    A. weighs more per foot
    B. has a smaller wall thickness
    C. has a larger inside diameter
    D. has more threads per inch.

24. If a 4-inch pipe is directly coupled to a 2-inch pipe and 16 gallons per minute are flowing through the 4-inch pipe, then the flow through the 2-inch pipe will be _____ gallons per minute.

    A. 4
    B. 8
    C. 16
    D. 32

25. A contractor is always complaining that he is being treated too harshly by an inspector. The BEST action for the inspector to take is to

   A. consider the complaints on their merit
   B. tell the contractor that he will not listen to any of his complaints
   C. *ride* the contractor until he stops complaining
   D. ignore the contractor's complaints

26. Each standpipe system control valve shall have a metal disk at least 3 inches in diameter securely attached to the valve.
The disk shall have white markings with a red background and should ALWAYS indicate

   A. the number assigned to it on the riser diagram for the standpipe system
   B. the direction to turn the valve to open and shut
   C. whether the water is good for drinking
   D. whether the valve is in the open or closed position

27. Riser control valves for standpipe systems shall, where practicable, be located

   A. outside the building in an easily accessible location
   B. as near as possible to the main control valves in the basement
   C. in the lobby of the building
   D. within a required stair enclosure serving the entrance floor

28. The BEST method to use to determine whether a large cast iron fitting is cracked is to

   A. visually examine the fitting for cracks
   B. put a water test on the fitting
   C. bang the fitting on concrete to see if it breaks
   D. *ring* the fitting with a hammer

29. Hydrostatic pressure tests for standpipe systems shall NORMALLY be performed for a period of at least

   A. 15 minutes   B. 1 hour
   C. 12 hours   D. 24 hours

30. The weight of a 6 foot length of 8-inch pipe which weighs 24.70 pounds per foot is _____ lbs.

   A. 148.2   B. 176.8   C. 197.6   D. 212.4

31. A *dresser* is MOST frequently used on _____ pipe.

   A. chrome-plated   B. brass
   C. lead   D. wrought iron

32. The cast iron fitting which is called a l/8th bend changes the direction of flow by an angle of

   A. 12 1/2°   B. 22 1/2°   C. 45°   D. 30°

33. Each service directly supplying a standpipe system or a fire pump shall be equipped with a control valve located

    A. in an exposed location within 1 ft. above the sidewalk
    B. in an exposed location within 2 ft. above the sidewalk
    C. under the sidewalk in a flush sidewalk box located within 1 ft. of the street line
    D. under the sidewalk in a flush sidewalk box located within 2 ft. of the street line

34. The MOST important requirement of a well-written report is that it should

    A. be very long and detailed
    B. have a proper heading
    C. be clear and brief
    D. have good punctuation

35. Gas service connections which supply gas to small residential buildings shall be provided with a regulator that will reduce the pressure of the gas to _____ psi.

    A. 4   B. 1   C. 2   D. 3

36. Each fixture trap in a building shall have a liquid seal of AT LEAST _____ inch(es).

    A. 4   B. 3   C. 2   D. 1

37. A pneumatic water supply system supplies water to the fixtures by means of _____ pressure.

    A. street   B. air   C. pump   D. steam

38. The opening pressure of the pressure relief valve on a boiler should be AT LEAST _____ pounds above the _____.

    A. 10; rated pressure of the boiler
    B. 25; rated pressure of the boiler
    C. 10; normal working pressure
    D. 25; normal working pressure

39. The plumbing term *pot piece* is GENERALLY used in connection with work involving the

    A. installation of water closets
    B. soldering of a lead cap
    C. caulking of a cast iron joint
    D. storing of fixtures and trim

40. The one of the following which is MOST likely to influence the minimum required size of a soil or waste stack is the

    A. number of offsets needed in the stack
    B. slope of the house drain
    C. height of the stack
    D. number and type of fixtures serviced by the stack

KEY (CORRECT ANSWERS)

1.	B	11.	B	21.	C	31.	C
2.	D	12.	A	22.	A	32.	C
3.	D	13.	C	23.	A	33.	D
4.	C	14.	D	24.	C	34.	C
5.	B	15.	B	25.	A	35.	A
6.	D	16.	A	26.	A	36.	C
7.	B	17.	B	27.	D	37.	B
8.	C	18.	D	28.	D	38.	D
9.	D	19.	B	29.	B	39.	C
10.	B	20.	B	30.	A	40.	D

EXAMINATION SECTION
TEST 1

DIRECTIONS: Each question or incomplete statement is followed by several suggested answers or completions. Select the one that BEST answers the question or completes the statement. *PRINT THE LETTER OF THE CORRECT ANSWER IN THE SPACE AT THE RIGHT.*

1. The MINIMUM number of appliance branch circuits required in the area comprising the kitchen, pantry, breakfast room, or dining alcove of dwelling occupancies is

    A. 1   B. 2   C. 3   D. 4

    1.____

2. In a living room, at least one receptacle outlet shall be provided *every* _____ feet.

    A. 15   B. 12   C. 10   D. 6

    2.____

3. Assume that new forty-watt fluorescent fixture ballasts which are not of the simple reactance type are being installed.
    According to code regulations governing fluorescent fixture ballast protection, these fixture ballasts

    A. cannot use non-renewable, non-resetting thermal protectors
    B. must be thermally protected
    C. can be protected by external exposed thermal protection
    D. cannot use (thermostatic) automatic resetting thermal protectors

    3.____

4. According to the code regulations on grounding of electrical systems, the neutral of a 4-wire, 3-phase A.C. system in an office building

    A. is grounded at the service entrance
    B. need not be grounded
    C. must be tied to the conduit system at each panel board
    D. is connected at each motor to a green grounding conductor

    4.____

5. With regard to the grounding of electrical systems, it is CORRECT to state that electrical systems

    A. must always be grounded
    B. must be provided with a ground detector, if ungrounded
    C. must always have a separate grounding conductor
    D. of less than fifty volts need not be grounded

    5.____

6. With regard to the position or arrangement of the disconnecting means of a motor, it is CORRECT to say that the disconnecting equipment

    A. must always be within the line of sight
    B. are always in the same enclosure as the motor controller
    C. must be on the motor frame
    D. can be arranged to be locked in the open position

    6.____

7. A 60-ampere subfeeder is connected to a 300-ampere main feeder. In order to properly protect the subfeeder,

    A. the protective device must be installed within one foot of the tap
    B. the protective device must be within five feet of the tap
    C. only fuses may be used
    D. only circuit breakers may be used

8. Assume that a three-phase feeder with its neutral is in a raceway. The *allowable* current capacity of the cable is _____ the appropriate tables in the code.

    A. greater than that obtained from
    B. 90 percent less than that obtained from
    C. the same as that obtained from
    D. 80 percent less than shown in

9. For rewiring existing raceways, the number of conductors permitted is _____ for new raceways.

    A. greater than
    B. the same as
    C. less than
    D. sixty-five percent greater than

10. The current capacity of copper bars is determined by using

    A. appropriate tables
    B. a current density of 100 amperes per sq. inch
    C. a current density of 500 amperes per sq. inch
    D. calculated short circuit forces

11. A special junction box is to be ordered to meet an unusual situation. The size of the box is determined PRIMARILY by the

    A. space available in which to locate the box
    B. location of the box
    C. material of which the box is made
    D. number and size of the wires running through or terminating in the box

12. When it is necessary to install three sets of parallel service feeders, the code requires that

    A. the conductors of each phase should be run in the same conduit
    B. the neutrals should be run in one conduit
    C. the conductors of each phase can be of greatly different lengths
    D. each phase conductor and the neutral conductor, if used, must be installed in each conduit

13. In order to pull a four-wire 250,000 cm RHW feeder into a conduit through a property line junction box, the type of lubricant that should be used is

    A. a heavy oil
    B. graphite or talc
    C. a light oil
    D. a light automotive grease

14. A 4"-conduit run changes its direction from horizontal to vertical and a pull box is installed at this point to facilitate fishing wire into the conduit.
For this purpose, it is BEST to place

   A. an elbow at the turn and install the box close by in the straight run of conduit
   B. the box at the turn, with the largest dimension in the horizontal direction
   C. the box at the turn, with the largest dimension in the vertical direction
   D. the box at the turn with the largest dimension at right angles to both the vertical and the horizontal conduits

14.____

15. The BEST way to attach a wire to a screw terminal is to

   A. place it straight under the screw head
   B. form a counterclockwise loop under the screw head
   C. form a clockwise loop under the screw head
   D. place the straight wire under the right side of the screw head

15.____

16. The MINIMUM number of wattmeters which may be used to measure the power in a delta-connected unbalanced three-phase load is

   A. 1   B. 2   C. 3   D. 4

16.____

17. An open-circuit test on a transformer is used to measure

   A. core losses
   B. copper losses
   C. windage and friction losses
   D. full-load efficiency

17.____

18. A meter that is used to measure the total energy consumed is a(n)

   A. demand meter   B. watt-hour meter
   C. ampere-hour meter   D. wattmeter

18.____

19. Assume that you are given a group of resistors with values ranging from 5 ohms to 10 megohms.
Of the following types of equipment, the one that you would use to sort them out is a(n)

   A. continuity checker made up of a battery and buzzer
   B. test lamp
   C. low-resistance voltmeter and battery
   D. ohmmeter

19.____

20. A 20:1 potential transformer is used to measure the voltage of a high voltage line.
If a voltmeter on the secondary of the transformer indicates 180 volts, the line voltage is MOST NEARLY _____ volts.

   A. 9   B. 360   C. 3600   D. 4000

20.____

21. A 50:1 current transformer in a feeder line has a 0-1 ammeter connected to its secondary.
If the meter indicates 0.5 amperes, the line current is MOST NEARLY _____ amperes.

   A. 0.01   B. 0.1   C. 2.5   D. 25

21.____

22. After a wiring installation is completed and it is found to be free of shorts and grounds, it *still* must be tested for

    A. dielectric strength
    B. arc-over voltage
    C. breakdown voltage
    D. insulation resistance

23. A voltmeter has a resistance of 1000 ohms on its 1-volt range. Its 250-volt range will have a resistance of MOST NEARLY _____ ohms.

    A. 250,000   B. 249,000   C. 25,000   D. 24,900

24. A voltmeter is marked 10,000 ohms per volt. It is used on its 150-volt range to measure a 100-volt source. The resistance of the voltmeter on this range is MOST NEARLY _____ ohms.

    A. 10,000   B. 100,000   C. 1,000,000   D. 1,500,000

25. A short-circuit test on a transformer is used to measure

    A. core losses
    B. copper losses
    C. stray power losses
    D. full load efficiency

KEY (CORRECT ANSWERS)

1. B
2. A
3. B
4. A
5. D

6. D
7. B
8. C
9. A
10. A

11. D
12. D
13. B
14. A
15. C

16. B
17. A
18. B
19. D
20. C

21. D
22. D
23. A
24. D
25. B

TEST 2

DIRECTIONS: Each question or incomplete statement is followed by several suggested answers or completions. Select the one that BEST answers the question or completes the statement. *PRINT THE LETTER OF THE CORRECT ANSWER IN THE SPACE AT THE RIGHT.*

1. The symbol S_4 on a plan indicates

    A. a four-way switch
    B. four switches
    C. signal number 4
    D. a switch for circuit number 4

    1.____

2. The symbol ⊖ on a plan stands for a

    A. single convenience outlet
    B. duplex convenience outlet
    C. male plug
    D. ceiling outlet

    2.____

3. A floor plan of light and power wiring is a

    A. detailed schematic showing the interconnection of all wiring involved
    B. detailed schematic showing color coding of all wiring interconnections for a given floor
    C. single line drawing showing wiring runs and the location of all outlets and runs for a given floor
    D. detailed layout of conduit runs showing all boxes and conduit connections for a given floor

    3.____

4. In order to determine from electrical plans the quantity of a particular size of conduit to be ordered,

    A. the distance of all runs of that particular size should be totaled
    B. the distance of all runs of that particular size should be totaled and increased by 5%
    C. no allowance should be made for vertical runs of that particular size
    D. count the number of boxes and multiply by an empirical factor for that particular size, obtained from experience

    4.____

5. Specifications for a store-and-office building specify a 2000-watt sign outlet over the entrance to each store, but nothing is indicated on the plans.
This means that

    A. the outlet must be installed by the contractor
    B. the outlet need not be installed
    C. an extra charge will be allowed for installing the outlet
    D. no additional switches or circuit breakers need be provided

    5.____

6. Assume that, in a certain contract, the plans as approved by the bureau of gas and electricity show number 10 AWG wires rated at 30 amperes supplying 16-ampere loads protected by 20-ampere circuit breakers.
   The PROPER action to be taken by contractor is that he

   A. can add additional loads up to 20 amperes
   B. can change the breakers to 30 amperes and increase the loads to 24 amperes
   C. must install the wiring in accordance with the plans
   D. can tell the owner that he can save him money by increasing the loads per circuit and reducing the number of circuits

7. The symbol shown at the right on a solenoid-controlled motor starting schematic indicates a
   A. variable capacitor and a fuse
   B. normally closed contact and a fuse
   C. normally closed contact and a circuit breaker
   D. thermal overload relay

8. A standard three-phase 208V motor contactor controls a pump motor for a water tower.
   In MOST common installations of this type, the float switch

   A. has contacts through which the motor current flows
   B. operates the contactor solenoid
   C. operates a relay which in turn operates the motor control solenoid
   D. controls a solid state switch

9. Plans show two multiple feeders each of 250 MCM size.
   The contractor proposes to install one set of 500 MCM size and claims that ample capacity is thereby obtained.
   As an inspector, you should

   A. not permit the installation
   B. permit the installation without further consultation
   C. permit the installation but write a report to your supervisor
   D. tell the contractor to obtain approval from the code revision and interpretation committee

10. The pushbutton control for a 10 HP motor USUALLY is a(n)

    A. on-off switch
    B. single-pole double-throw switch
    C. double-pole double-throw switch
    D. momentary-contact switch in series with a normally closed spring-loaded switch

11. The president of a tenant's association calls the bureau of gas and electricity and complains about dangerous open wiring. You are assigned to investigate this complaint.
    The BEST procedure for you to follow is to

    A. inspect the premises before taking any further action
    B. immediately request that the appropriate group at the realty board repair the wiring
    C. call the president, at once, to assure him or her that the wiring will be fixed immediately
    D. immediately file a code violation against the premises

12. The bureau of gas and electricity receives a complaint of a street light shining in someone's window.
    As the inspector assigned to the complaint, you should

    A. immediately order a shield placed on the offending light
    B. tell the complainant that the problem will be completely resolved
    C. tell the complainant that the light is necessary for safety and that nothing can be done
    D. carefully check the location mentioned in the complaint, especially at night, before making any report or recommendations

13. An electrical contractor explains to you that field conditions prevent him from making an installation in accordance with the code.
    Your FIRST action should be to

    A. insist that the work be done in accordance with the code immediately
    B. tell the contractor that you will take it upon yourself to approve the change if the work can be done safely by the contractor's men
    C. file a violation against the work
    D. tell the contractor to apply to the code revision and interpretation committee, while you make a complete report and recommendation to your superior

14. You are called by an irate individual complaining that he has received an electrical bill that is excessive compared to his bill for the same period one year ago. A PROPER tactful procedure is to

    A. tell the individual that your department has no jurisdiction and hang up
    B. carefully listen to the individual and suggest that the complaint be taken to the utility and indicate that the last resort is the Public Service Commission
    C. tell the individual to have his wiring checked by an electrician
    D. agree with the individual, and suggest that only part of the bill be paid and that a letter pointing out the error be sent to the electric company

15. An irate person complains to you about the waste of public money because the lights on a portion of a highway are on during the day.
    Your response should be to

    A. agree with the person, but tell him that this matter is not in the bureau's jurisdiction and that nothing can be done to remedy the condition
    B. explain that payment to the electrical utility for the lighting is made on a scheduled basis, and that the matter will be corrected as soon as possible
    C. refer him to someone else
    D. refer him to the electrical utility

16. For safe work in buildings, the code states that portable hand-held drills and saws connected by cord and plug

    A. need have only two wires in the cord
    B. must always have a ground connection to exposed non-current carrying metal parts
    C. can be used to drill into live bus-bars
    D. need not be grounded if protected by an approved system of double insulation and distinctly so marked

17. A newly installed motor and control with the disconnect not in the line of sight are to be inspected.
Before starting the inspection, it is ESSENTIAL to

   A. set the motor feeder circuit breaker to off
   B. press the control off button
   C. lock the motor disconnect in the off position
   D. remove the equipment drive belt

18. In order to find a blown cartridge fuse on a three-phase 208/120 volt A.C. panelboard, it is BEST to use

   A. fingers across each fuse
   B. a small neon test lamp connected from the line side of each fuse to ground
   C. a 50-watt 120-volt test lamp placed from ground to the load side of each fuse in turn
   D. an ohmmeter across each fuse on the panelboard

19. In order to pull wires into a conduit which terminates in a live panelboard supplied by 208/120V A.C., it is BEST to use a

   A. non-metallic fishline
   B. length of galvanized steel wire
   C. steel fish tape
   D. length of steel chain

20. A branch circuit which is protected by a plug fuse is to be modified.
In order to do the job safely, it is BEST to

   A. turn the circuit switch to off before starting work
   B. loosen the fuse before starting work
   C. remove the fuse entirely before starting work
   D. work with the circuit alive

21. The current in a feeder is to be measured by using a clamp-on current transformer and a separate ammeter.
Before placing the current transformer over the feeder,

   A. no special precautions need be taken
   B. the transformer secondary must be short-circuited
   C. the feeder must be disconnected
   D. the transformer secondary must be open-circuited

22. A workman is found to be in contact with live electrical equipment.
The FIRST thing that a rescuer must do is to

   A. apply artificial respiration
   B. grab the victim around the waist and remove him from the equipment
   C. call an ambulance
   D. disconnect the equipment by any means or remove the victim using rubber gloves

23. Of the following types of wiring methods, the one which must be used in a Class I hazardous location is

    A. electrical metallic tubing with pressure fittings
    B. armored cable
    C. non-metallic sheathed cable
    D. rigid conduit with explosion-proof joints and fittings

24. An electrician falls off a scaffold. He is semi-conscious and breathing. The FIRST thing that should be done is to

    A. move the victim to a sheltered place
    B. force whiskey or brandy into his mouth
    C. start artificial respiration
    D. keep the injured person lying down in a comfortable position with his lead level with his body

25. Of the following statements concerning the installation of lamp holding devices in basements, the one that is CORRECT is that they

    A. shall be porcelain or bakelite
    B. shall not be key-operated
    C. may have metal shells
    D. shall not be pullchain-operated

KEY (CORRECT ANSWERS)

1. A		11. A	
2. B		12. D	
3. C		13. D	
4. B		14. B	
5. A		15. B	
6. C		16. D	
7. D		17. C	
8. B		18. C	
9. A		19. A	
10. D		20. C	

21. B
22. D
23. D
24. D
25. A

PREPARING WRITTEN MATERIAL

PARAGRAPH REARRANGEMENT
COMMENTARY

The sentences that follow are in scrambled order. You are to rearrange them in proper order and indicate the letter choice containing the correct answer at the space at the right.

Each group of sentences in this section is actually a paragraph presented in scrambled order. Each sentence in the group has a place in that paragraph; no sentence is to be left out. You are to read each group of sentences and decide upon the best order in which to put the sentences so as to form a well-organized paragraph.

The questions in this section measure the ability to solve a problem when all the facts relevant to its solution are not given.

More specifically, certain positions of responsibility and authority require the employee to discover connection between events sometimes, apparently, unrelated. In order to do this, the employee will find it necessary to correctly infer that unspecified events have probably occurred or are likely to occur. This ability becomes especially important when action must be taken on incomplete information.

Accordingly, these questions require competitors to choose among several suggested alternatives, each of which presents a different sequential arrangement of the events. Competitors must choose the MOST logical of the suggested sequences.

In order to do so, they may be required to draw on general knowledge to infer missing concepts or events that are essential to sequencing the given events. Competitors should be careful to infer only what is essential to the sequence. The plausibility of the wrong alternatives will always require the inclusion of unlikely events or of additional chains of events which are NOT essential to sequencing the given events.

It's very important to remember that you are looking for the best of the four possible choices, and that the best choice of all may not even be one of the answers you're given to choose from.

There is no one right way to solve these problems. Many people have found it helpful to first write out the order of the sentences, as they would have arranged them, on their scrap paper before looking at the possible answers. If their optimum answer is there, this can save them some time. If it isn't, this method can still give insight into solving the problem. Others find it most helpful to just go through each of the possible choices, contrasting each as they go along. You should use whatever method feels comfortable and works for you.

While most of these types of questions are not that difficult, we've added a higher percentage of the difficult type, just to give you more practice. Usually there are only one or two questions on this section that contain such subtle distinctions that you're unable to answer confidently. And you then may find yourself stuck deciding between two possible choices, neither of which you're sure about.

EXAMINATION SECTION
TEST 1

DIRECTIONS: The sentences that follow are in scrambled order. You are to rearrange them in proper order and indicate the letter choice containing the correct answer. *PRINT THE LETTER OF THE CORRECT ANSWER IN THE SPACE AT THE RIGHT.*

1. Below are four statements labeled W, X, Y and Z. 1.____
   W. He was a strict and fanatic drillmaster.
   X. The word is always used in a derogatory sense and generally shows resentment and anger on the part of the user.
   Y. It is from the name of this Frenchman that we derive our English word, martinet.
   Z. Jean Martinet was the Inspector-General of Infantry during the reign of King Louis XIV.
   The PROPER order in which these sentences should be placed in a paragraph is:
   A. X, Z, W, Y   B. X, Z, Y, W   C. Z, W, Y, X   D. Z, Y, W, X

2. In the following paragraph, the sentences, which are numbered, have been jumbled. 2.____
   I. Since then it has undergone changes.
   II. It was incorporated in 1955 under the laws of the State of New York.
   III. Its primary purposes, a cleaner city, has, however, remained the same.
   IV. The Citizens Committee works in cooperation with the Mayor's Inter-departmental Committee for a Clean City. 3.____
   The order in which these sentences should be arranged to form a well-organized paragraph is:
   A. II, IV, I, III   B. III, IV, I, II   C. IV, II, I, III   D. IV, III, II, I

Questions 3-5.

DIRECTIONS: The sentences listed below are part of a meaningful paragraph but they are not given in their proper order. You are to decide what would be the BEST order in which to put the sentences so as to form a well-organized paragraph. Each sentence has a place in the paragraph; there are no extra sentences. You are then to answer Questions 3 through 5 inclusive on the basis of your rearrangements of these scrambled sentences into a properly organized paragraph.

In 1887 some insurance companies organized an Inspection Department to advise their clients on all phases of fire prevention and protection. Probably this has been due to the smaller annual fire losses in Great Britain than in the United States. It tests various fire prevention devices and appliances and determines manufacturing hazards and their safeguards. Fire research began earlier in the United States and is more advanced than in Great Britain. Later they established a laboratory specializing in electrical, mechanical, hydraulic, and chemical fields.

2 (#1)

3. When the five sentences are arranged in proper order, the paragraph starts with the sentence which begins 3.____
   A. "In 1887..."   B. "Probably this..."   C. "It tests..."
   D. "Fire research..."   E. "Later they..."

4. In the last sentence listed above, "they" refers to 4.____
   A. the insurance companies
   B. the United States and Great Britain
   C. the Inspection Department
   D. clients
   E. technicians

5. When the above paragraph is properly arranged, it ends with the words 5.____
   A. "...and protection."   B. "...the United States."
   C. "...their safeguards."   D. "...in Great Britain."
   E. "...chemical fields."

KEY (CORRECT ANSWERS)

1. C
2. C
3. D
4. A
5. C

TEST 2

DIRECTIONS: In each of the questions numbered I through V, several sentences are given. For each question, choose as your answer the group of number that represents the MOST logical order of these sentences if they were arranged in paragraph form. *PRINT THE LETTER OF THE CORRECT ANSWER IN THE SPACE AT THE RIGHT.*

1. I. It is established when one shows that the landlord has prevented the tenant's enjoyment of his interest in the property leased.
    II. Constructive eviction is the result of a breach of the covenant of quiet enjoyment implied in all leases.
    III. In some parts of the United States, it is not complete until the tenant vacates within a reasonable time.
    IV. Generally, the acts must be of such serious and permanent character as to deny the tenant the enjoyment of his possessing rights.
    V. In this event, upon abandonment of the premises, the tenant's liability for that ceases.
    The CORRECT answer is:
    A. II, I, IV, III, V
    B. V, II, III, I, IV
    C. IV, III, I, II, V
    D. I, III, V, IV, II

    1.____

2. I. The powerlessness before private and public authorities that is the typical experience of the slum tenant is reminiscent of the situation of blue-collar workers all through the nineteenth century.
    II. Similarly, in recent years, this chapter of history has been reopened by anti-poverty groups which have attempted to organize slum tenants to enable them to bargain collectively with their landlords about the conditions of their tenancies.
    III. It is familiar history that many of the worker remedied their condition by joining together and presenting their demands collectively.
    IV. Like the workers, tenants are forced by the conditions of modern life into substantial dependence on these who possess great political aid and economic power.
    V. What's more, the very fact of dependence coupled with an absence of education and self-confidence makes them hesitant and unable to stand up for what they need from those in power.
    The CORRECT answer is:
    A. V, IV, I, II, III
    B. II, III, I, V, IV
    C. III, I, V, IV, II
    D. I, IV, V, III, II

    2.____

3. I. A railroad, for example, when not acting as a common carrier may contract away responsibility for its own negligence.
    II. As to a landlord, however, no decision has been found relating to the legal effect of a clause shifting the statutory duty of repair to the tenant.
    III. The courts have not passed on the validity of clauses relieving the landlord of this duty and liability.
    IV. They have, however, upheld the validity of exculpatory clauses in other types of contracts.

    3.____

81

V. Housing regulations impose a duty upon the landlord to maintain leased premises in safe condition.
VI. As another example, a bailee may limit his liability except for gross negligence, willful acts, or fraud.

The CORRECT answer is:
A. II, I, VI, IV, III, V
B. I, III, IV, V, VI, II
C. III, V, I, IV, II, VI
D. V, III, IV, I, VI, II

4.
I. Since there are only samples in the building, retail or consumer sales are generally eschewed by mart occupants, and in some instances, rigid controls are maintained to limit entrance to the mart only to those persons engaged in retailing.
II. Since World War I, in many larger cities, there has developed a new type of property, called the mart building.
III. It can, therefore, be used by wholesalers and jobbers for the display of sample merchandise.
IV. This type of building is most frequently a multi-storied, finished interior property which is a cross between a retail arcade and a loft building.
V. This limitation enables the mart occupants to ship the orders from another location after the retailer or dealer makes his selection from the samples.

The CORRECT answer is:
A. II, IV, III, I, V
B. IV, III, V, I, II
C. I, III, II, IV, V
D. I, IV, II, III, V

5.
I. In general, staff-line friction reduces the distinctive contribution of staff personnel.
II. The conflicts, however, introduce an uncontrolled element into the managerial system.
III. On the other hand, the natural resistance of the line to staff innovations probably usefully restrains over-eager efforts to apply untested procedures on a large scale.
IV. Under such conditions, it is difficult to know when valuable ideas are being sacrificed.
V. The relatively weak position of staff, requiring accommodation to the line, tends to restrict their ability to engage in free, experimental innovation.

The CORRECT answer is:
A. IV, II, III, I, V
B. I, V, III, II, IV
C. V, III, I, II, IV
D. II, I, IV, V, III

KEY (CORRECT ANSWERS)

1. A
2. D
3. D
4. A
5. B

TEST 3

DIRECTIONS: Questions 1 through 4 consist of six sentences which can be arranged in a logical sequence. For each question, select the choice which places the numbered sentences in the MOST logical sequent. *PRINT THE LETTER OF THE CORRECT ANSWER IN THE SPACE AT THE RIGHT.*

1.
   I. The burden of proof as to each issue is determined before trial and remains upon the same party throughout the trial.
   II. The jury is at liberty to believe one witness' testimony as against a number of contradictory witnesses.
   III. In a civil case, the party bearing the burden of proof is required to prove his contention by a fair preponderance of the evidence.
   IV. However, it must be noted that a fair preponderance of evidence does not necessarily mean a greater number of witnesses.
   V. The burden of proof is the burden which rests upon one of the parties to an action to persuade the trier of the facts, generally the jury, that a proposition he asserts is true.
   VI. If the evidence is equally balanced, or if it leaves the jury in such doubt as to be unable to decide the controversy either way, judgment must be given against the party upon whom the burden of proof rests.
   The CORRECT answer is:
   A. III, II, V, IV, I, VI
   B. I, II, VI, V, III, IV
   C. III, IV, V, I, II, VI
   D. V, I, III, VI, IV, II

   1.____

2.
   I. If a parent is without assets and is unemployed, he cannot be convicted of the crime of non-support of a child.
   II. The term "sufficient ability" has been held to mean sufficient financial ability.
   III. It does not matter if his unemployment is by choice or unavoidable circumstances.
   IV. If he fails to take any steps at all, he may be liable to prosecution for endangering the welfare of a child.
   V. Under the penal law, a parent is responsible for the support of his minor child only if the parent is "of sufficient ability."
   VI. An indigent parent may meet his obligation by borrowing money or by seeking aid under the provisions of the Social Welfare Law.
   The CORRECT answer is:
   A. VI, I, V, III, II, IV
   B. I, III, V, II, IV, VI
   C. V, II, I, III, VI, IV
   D. I, VI, IV, V, II, III

   2.____

3.
   I. Consider, for example, the case of a rabble rouser who urges a group of twenty people to go out and break the windows of a nearby factory.
   II. Therefore, the law fills the indicated gap with the crime of inciting to riot.
   III. A person is considered guilty of inciting to riot when he urges ten or more persons to engage in tumultuous and violent conduct of a kind likely to create public alarm.
   IV. However, if he has not obtained the cooperation of at least four people, he cannot be charged with unlawful assembly.

   3.____

V. The charge of inciting to riot was added to the law to cover types of conduct which cannot be classified as either the crime of "riot" or the crime of "unlawful assembly."
VI. If he acquires the acquiescence of at least four of them, he is guilty of unlawful assembly even if the project does not materialize.

The CORRECT answer is:
A. III, V, I, VI, IV, II
B. V, I, IV, VI, II, III
C. III, IV, I, V, II, VI
D. V, I, IV, VI, III, II

4.
I. If, however, the rebuttal evidence presents an issue of credibility, it is for the jury to determine whether the presumption has, in fact, been destroyed.
II. Once sufficient evidence to the contrary is introduced, the presumption disappears from the trial.
III. The effect of a presumption is to place the burden upon the adversary to come forward with evidence to rebut the presumption.
IV. When a presumption is overcome and ceases to exist in the case, the fact or facts which gave rise to the presumption still remain.
V. Whether a presumption has been overcome is ordinarily a question for the court.
VI. Such information may furnish a basis for a logical inference.

The CORRECT answer is:
A. IV, VI, II, V, I, III
B. III, II, V, I, IV, VI
C. V, III, VI, IV, II, I
D. V, IV, I, II, VI, III

KEY (CORRECT ANSWERS)

1. D
2. C
3. A
4. B

PREPARING WRITTEN MATERIAL
EXAMINATION SECTION
TEST 1

DIRECTIONS: Each of the sentences in this test may be classified under one of the following four categories:
- A. Faulty because of incorrect grammar or word usage
- B. Faulty because of incorrect punctuation
- C. Faulty because of incorrect capitalization or incorrect spelling
- D. Correct

Examine each sentence carefully to determine under which of the above four options it is best classified. Then, in the space to the right, print the capital letter preceding the option which is the BEST of the four suggested above. (Note that each faulty sentence contains but one type of error. Consider a sentence to be correct if it contains none of the types of errors mentioned, even though there may be other correct ways of expressing the same thought.)

1. He sent the notice to the clerk who you hired yesterday. 1.____

2. It must be admitted, however that you were not informed of this change. 2.____

3. Only the employee who have served in this grade for at least two years are eligible for promotion. 3.____

4. The work was divided equally between she and Mary. 4.____

5. He thought that you were not available at that time. 5.____

6. When the messenger returns; please give him this package. 6.____

7. The new secretary prepared, typed, addressed, and delivered, the notices. 7.____

8. Walking into the room, his desk can be seen at the rear. 8.____

9. Although John has worked here longer than She, he produces a smaller amount of work. 9.____

10. She said she could of typed this report yesterday. 10.____

11. Neither one of these procedures are adequate for the efficient performance of this task. 11.____

12. The typewriter is the tool of the typist; the cash register, the tool of the cashier. 12.____

85

13. "The assignment must be completed as soon as possible" said the supervisor. 13.____

14. As you know, office handbooks are issued to all new Employees. 14.____

15. Writing a speech is sometimes easier than to deliver it before an audience. 15.____

16. Mr. Brown our accountant, will audit the accounts next week. 16.____

17. Give the assignment to whomever is able to do it most efficiently. 17.____

18. The supervisor expected either your or I to file these reports. 18.____

KEY (CORRECT ANSWERS)

1.	A	11.	A
2.	B	12.	C
3.	D	13.	B
4.	A	14.	C
5.	D	15.	A
6.	B	16.	B
7.	B	17.	A
8.	A	18.	A
9.	C		
10.	A		

TEST 2

DIRECTIONS: Each of the sentences in this test may be classified under one of the following four categories:
- A. Faulty because of incorrect grammar or word usage
- B. Faulty because of incorrect punctuation
- C. Faulty because of incorrect capitalization or incorrect spelling
- D. Correct

Examine each sentence carefully to determine under which of the above four options it is best classified. Then, in the space to the right, print the capital letter preceding the option which is the BEST of the four suggested above. (Note that each faulty sentence contains but one type of error. Consider a sentence to be correct if it contains none of the types of errors mentioned, even though there may be other correct ways of expressing the same thought.)

1. The fire apparently started in the storeroom, which is usually locked. 1._____
2. On approaching the victim, two bruises were noticed by this officer. 2._____
3. The officer, who was there examined the report with great care. 3._____
4. Each employee in the office had a seperate desk. 4._____
5. All employees including members of the clerical staff, were invited to the lecture. 5._____
6. The suggested Procedure is similar to the one now in use. 6._____
7. No one was more pleased with the new procedure than the chauffeur. 7._____
8. He tried to persaude her to change the procedure. 8._____
9. The total of the expenses charged to petty cash were high. 9._____
10. An understanding between him and I was finally reached. 10._____

KEY (CORRECT ANSWERS)

1.	D	6.	C
2.	A	7.	D
3.	B	8.	C
4.	C	9.	A
5.	B	10.	A

TEST 3

DIRECTIONS: Each of the sentences in this test may be classified under one of the following four categories:
   A. Faulty because of incorrect grammar or word usage
   B. Faulty because of incorrect punctuation
   C. Faulty because of incorrect capitalization or incorrect spelling
   D. Correct

Examine each sentence carefully to determine under which of the above four options it is best classified. Then, in the space to the right, print the capital letter preceding the option which is the BEST of the four suggested above. (Note that each faulty sentence contains but one type of error. Consider a sentence to be correct if it contains none of the types of errors mentioned, even though there may be other correct ways of expressing the same thought.)

1. They told both he and I that the prisoner had escaped. 1.____

2. Any superior officer, who, disregards the just complaint of his subordinates, is remiss in the performance of his duty. 2.____

3. Only those members of the national organization who resided in the Middle West attended the conference in Chicago. 3.____

4. We told him to give the national organization assignment to whoever was available. 4.____

5. Please do not disappoint and embarass us by not appearing in court. 5.____

6. Although the office's speech proved to be entertaining, the topic was not relevent to the main theme of the conference. 6.____

7. In February all new officers attended a training course in which they were learned in their principal duties and the fundamental operating procedure of the department. 7.____

8. I personally seen inmate Jones threaten inmates Smith and Green with bodily harm if they refused to participate in the plot. 8.____

9. To the layman, who on a chance visit to the prison observes everything functioning smoothly, the maintenance of prison discipline may seem to be a relatively easily realizable objective. 9.____

10. The prisoners in cell block fourty were forbidden to sit on the cell cots during the recreation hour. 10.____

KEY (CORRECT ANSWERS)

1. A   6. C
2. B   7. A
3. C   8. A
4. D   9. D
5. C   10. C

TEST 4

DIRECTIONS: Each of the sentences in this test may be classified under one of the following four categories:
- A. Faulty because of incorrect grammar or word usage
- B. Faulty because of incorrect punctuation
- C. Faulty because of incorrect capitalization or incorrect spelling
- D. Correct

Examine each sentence carefully to determine under which of the above four options it is best classified. Then, in the space to the right, print the capital letter preceding the option which is the BEST of the four suggested above. (Note that each faulty sentence contains but one type of error. Consider a sentence to be correct if it contains none of the types of errors mentioned, even though there may be other correct ways of expressing the same thought.)

1. I cannot encourage you any. 1._____
2. You always look well in those sort of clothes. 2._____
3. Shall we go to the park? 3._____
4. The man whome he introduced was Mr. Carey. 4._____
5. She saw the letter laying here this morning. 5._____
6. It should rain before the Afternoon is over. 6._____
7. They have already went home. 7._____
8. That Jackson will be elected is evident. 8._____
9. He does not hardly approve of us. 9._____
10. It was he, who won the prize. 10._____

KEY (CORRECT ANSWERS)

1. A   6. C
2. A   7. A
3. D   8. D
4. C   9. A
5. A   10. B

TEST 5

DIRECTIONS: Each of the sentences in this test may be classified under one of the following four categories:
  A. Faulty because of incorrect grammar or word usage
  B. Faulty because of incorrect punctuation
  C. Faulty because of incorrect capitalization or incorrect spelling
  D. Correct

Examine each sentence carefully to determine under which of the above four options it is best classified. Then, in the space to the right, print the capital letter preceding the option which is the BEST of the four suggested above. (Note that each faulty sentence contains but one type of error. Consider a sentence to be correct if it contains none of the types of errors mentioned, even though there may be other correct ways of expressing the same thought.)

1. Shall we go to the park.   1.____
2. They are, alike, in this particular way.   2.____
3. They gave the poor man sume food when he knocked on the door.   3.____
4. I regret the loss caused by the error.   4.____
5. The students' will have a new teacher.   5.____
6. They sweared to bring out all the facts.   6.____
7. He decided to open a branch store on 33rd street.   7.____
8. His speed is equal and more than that of a racehorse.   8.____
9. He felt very warm on that Summer day.   9.____
10. He was assisted by his friend, who lives in the next house.   10.____

KEY (CORRECT ANSWERS)

1.	B	6.	A
2.	B	7.	C
3.	C	8.	A
4.	D	9.	C
5.	B	10.	D

TEST 6

DIRECTIONS: Each of the sentences in this test may be classified under one of the following four categories:
- A. Faulty because of incorrect grammar or word usage
- B. Faulty because of incorrect punctuation
- C. Faulty because of incorrect capitalization or incorrect spelling
- D. Correct

Examine each sentence carefully to determine under which of the above four options it is best classified. Then, in the space to the right, print the capital letter preceding the option which is the BEST of the four suggested above. (Note that each faulty sentence contains but one type of error. Consider a sentence to be correct if it contains none of the types of errors mentioned, even though there may be other correct ways of expressing the same thought.)

1. The climate of New York is colder than California.   1.____
2. I shall wait for you on the corner.   2.____
3. Did we see the boy who, we think, is the leader.   3.____
4. Being a modest person, John seldom talks about his invention.   4.____
5. The gang is called the smith street bos.   5.____
6. He seen the man break into the store.   6.____
7. We expected to lay still there for quite a while.   7.____
8. He is considered to be the Leader of his organization.   8.____
9. Although I recieved an invitation, I won't go.   9.____
10. The letter must be here some place.   10.____

KEY (CORRECT ANSWERS)

1.	A	6.	A
2.	D	7.	A
3.	B	8.	C
4.	D	9.	C
5.	C	10.	A

TEST 7

DIRECTIONS: Each of the sentences in this test may be classified under one of the following four categories:
  A. Faulty because of incorrect grammar or word usage
  B. Faulty because of incorrect punctuation
  C. Faulty because of incorrect capitalization or incorrect spelling
  D. Correct

Examine each sentence carefully to determine under which of the above four options it is best classified. Then, in the space to the right, print the capital letter preceding the option which is the BEST of the four suggested above. (Note that each faulty sentence contains but one type of error. Consider a sentence to be correct if it contains none of the types of errors mentioned, even though there may be other correct ways of expressing the same thought.)

1. I though it to be he. 1.____
2. We expect to remain here for a long time. 2.____
3. The committee was agreed. 3.____
4. Two-thirds of the building are finished. 4.____
5. The water was froze. 5.____
6. Everyone of the salesmen must supply their own car. 6.____
7. Who is the author of Gone With the Wind? 7.____
8. He marched on and declaring that he would never surrender. 8.____
9. Who shall I say called? 9.____
10. Everyone has left but they. 10.____

KEY (CORRECT ANSWERS)

1. A   6. A
2. D   7. B
3. D   8. A
4. A   9. D
5. A   10. D

TEST 8

DIRECTIONS: Each of the sentences in this test may be classified under one of the following four categories:
- A. Faulty because of incorrect grammar or word usage
- B. Faulty because of incorrect punctuation
- C. Faulty because of incorrect capitalization or incorrect spelling
- D. Correct

Examine each sentence carefully to determine under which of the above four options it is best classified. Then, in the space to the right, print the capital letter preceding the option which is the BEST of the four suggested above. (Note that each faulty sentence contains but one type of error. Consider a sentence to be correct if it contains none of the types of errors mentioned, even though there may be other correct ways of expressing the same thought.)

1. Who did we give the order to? 1.____
2. Send your order in immediately. 2.____
3. I believe I paid the Bill. 3.____
4. I have not met but one person. 4.____
5. Why aren't Tom, and Fred, going to the dance? 5.____
6. What reason is there for him not going? 6.____
7. The seige of Malta was a tremendous event. 7.____
8. I was there yesterday I assure you 8.____
9. Your ukulele is better than mine. 9.____
10. No one was there only Mary. 10.____

KEY (CORRECT ANSWERS)

1.	A	6.	A
2.	D	7.	C
3.	C	8.	B
4.	A	9.	C
5.	B	10.	A

TEST 9

DIRECTIONS: In each of the following groups of sentences, one of the four sentences is faulty in grammar, punctuation, or capitalization. Select the INCORRECT sentence in each case.

1. A. If you had stood at home and done your homework, you would not have failed in arithmetic.
   B. Her affected manner annoyed every member of the audience.
   C. How will the new law affect our income taxes?
   D. The plants were not affected by the long, cold winter, but they succumbed to the drought of summer.

   1.____

2. A. He is one of the most able men who have been in the Senate.
   B. It is he who is to blame for the lamentable mistake.
   C. Haven't you a helpful suggestion to make at this time?
   D. The money was robbed from the blind man's cup.

   2.____

3. A. The amount of children in this school is steadily increasing.
   B. After taking an apple from the table, she went out to play.
   C. He borrowed a dollar from me.
   D. I had hoped my brother would arrive before me.

   3.____

4. A. Whom do you think I hear from every week?
   B. Who do you think is the right man for the job?
   C. Who do you think I found in the room?
   D. He is the man whom we considered a good candidate for the presidency.

   4.____

5. A. Quietly the puppy laid down before the fireplace.
   B. You have made your bed; now lie in it.
   C. I was badly sunburned because I had lain too long in the sun.
   D. I laid the doll on the bed and left the room.

   5.____

KEY (CORRECT ANSWERS)

1. A
2. D
3. A
4. C
5. A

BUILDING ASPECTS OF A HOUSING INSPECTION

CONTENTS

		Page
I.	Background Factors	1
II.	Housing Construction Terminology	1
III.	Structure	4
IV.	Discussion of Inspection Techniques	15
V.	Noise as an Environmental Stress	17

BUILDING ASPECTS OF A HOUSING INSPECTION

The principle function of a house is to furnish protection from the elements. In its current stage, however, our civilization requires that a home provide not only shelter but also privacy, safety, and reasonable protection of our physical and mental health. A living facility that fails to offer these essentials through adequately designed and properly maintained interiors and exteriors cannot be termed "healthful housing."

I. Background Factors

In this chapter, a building will be considered in terms of its major components: heating, plumbing, and electrical systems. Each of these items will be examined in detail in future chapters. Attention will be given in this chapter to the portions of a building not visible upon completion of the ceiling, roof, and interior and exterior walls in order to give the reader an understanding of generally accepted construction practices. Emphasis, however, will be placed upon the visible interior and exterior parts of a completed dwelling that have a bearing on the soundness, state of repair, and safety of the dwelling both during intended use and in the event of a fire. These are some of the elements that the housing inspector must examine when making a thorough housing inspection.

II. Housing Construction Terminology

(Key to Component Parts Numbered in Figure 1)

A Fireplace

1 **Chimney** - A vertical masonry shaft of reinforced concrete or other approved non-combustible, heat resisting material enclosing one or more flues. It removes the products of combustion from solid, liquid, or gaseous fuel.

2 **Flue Liner** - The flue is the hole in the chimney. The liner, usually of terra cotta, protects the brick from harmful smoke gases.

3 **Chimney Cap** - This top is generally of concrete. It protects the brick from weather.

4 **Chimney Flashing** - Sheet-metal flashing provides a tight joint between chimney and roof.

5 **Firebrick** - An ordinary brick cannot withstand the heat of direct fire, and so special firebrick is used to line the fireplace.

6 **Ash Dump** - A trap door to let the ashes drop to a pit below, from where they may be easily removed.

7 **Cleanout Door** - The door to the ash pit or the bottom of a chimney through which the chimney can be cleaned.

8 **Chimney Breast** - The inside face or front of a fireplace chimney.

9 **Hearth** - The floor of a fireplace that extends into the room for safety purposes.

B Roof

10 **Ridge** - The top intersection of two opposite adjoining roof surfaces.

11 **Ridge Board** - The board that follows along under the ridge.

12 **Roof Rafters** - The structural members that support the roof.

13 **Collar Beam** - Really not a beam at all. A tie that keeps the roof from spreading. Connects similar rafters on opposite side of roof.

14 **Roof Insulation** - An insulating material (usually rock wool or fiberglas) in a blanket form placed between the roof rafters for the purpose of keeping a house warm in the winter, cool in the summer.

15 **Roof Sheathing** - The boards that provide the base for the finished roof.

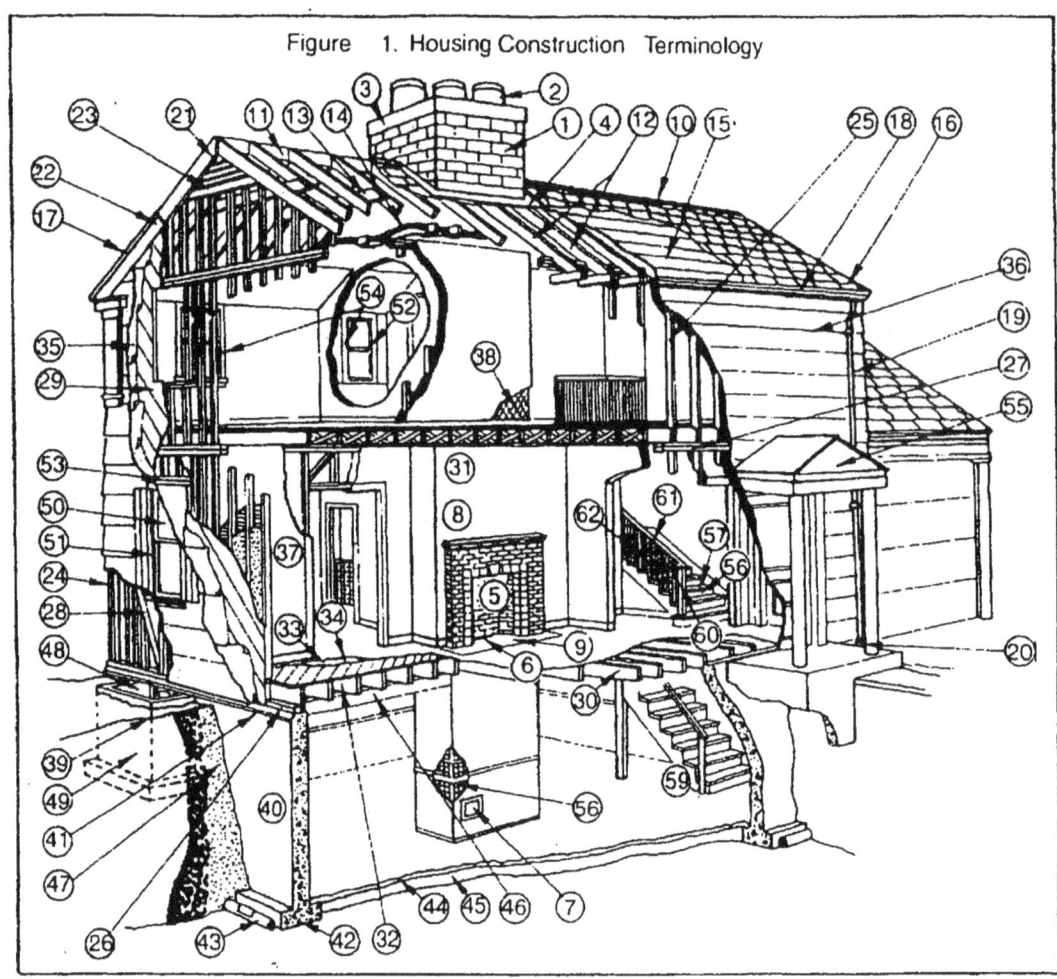

Figure 1. Housing Construction Terminology

16 **Roofing** - The wood, asphalt, or asbestos shingles - or tile, slate or metal - that form the outer protection against the weather.

17 **Cornice** - A decorative element made up of molded members usually placed at or near the top of an exterior or interior wall.

18 **Gutter** - The trough that gathers rainwater from a roof.

19 **Downspouts** - The pipe that leads the water down from the gutter.

20 **Storm Sewer Tile** - The underground pipe that receives the water from the downspouts and carries it to the sewer.

21 **Gable** - The triangular end of a building with a sloping roof.

22 **Barage Board** - The fascia or board at the gable just under the edge of the roof.

23 **Louvers** - A series of slanted slots arranged to keep out rain, yet allow ventilation.

C Walls and Floors

24 **Corner Post** - The vertical member at the corner of the frame, made up to receive inner and outer covering materials.

25 **Studs** - The vertical wood members of the house, usually 2 X 4's generally spaced every 16 inches.

26 **Sill** - The board that is laid first on the foundation, and on which the frame rests.

27 **Plate** - The board laid across the top ends of the studs to hold them even and rigid.

28 **Corner Bracing** - Diagonal strips to keep the frame square and plumb.

29 **Sheathing** - The first layer of outer wall covering nailed to the studs.

30 **Joist** - The structural members or beams that hold up the floor or ceiling, usually 2 X 10's or 2 X 12's spaced 16 inches apart.

31 **Bridging** - Cross bridging or solid. Members at the middle or third points of joist spans to brace one to the next and to prevent their twisting.

32 **Subflooring** - The rough boards that are laid over the joist. Usually laid diagonally.

33 **Flooring Paper** - A felt paper laid on the rough floor to stop air infiltration and, to some extent, noise.

34 **Finish Flooring** - Usually hardwood, of tongued and grooved strips.

35 **Building Paper** - Paper placed outside the sheathing, not as a vapor barrier, but to prevent water and air from leaking in. Building paper is also used as a tarred felt under shingles or siding to keep out moisture or wind.

36 **Beveled Siding** - Sometimes called clapboards, with a thick butt and a thin upper edge lapped to shed water.

37 **Wall Insulation** - A blanket of wool or reflective foil placed inside the walls.

38 **Metal Lath** - A mesh made from sheet metal onto which plaster is applied.

D **Foundation and Basement**

39 **Finished Grade Line** - The top of the ground at the foundation.

40 **Foundation Wall** - The wall of poured concrete (shown) or concrete blocks that rests on the footing and supports the remainder of the house.

41 **Termite Shield** - A metal baffle to prevent termites from entering the frame.

42 **Footing** - The concrete pad that carries the entire weight of the house upon the earth.

43 **Footing Drain Tile** - A pipe with cracks at the joints to allow underground water to drain in and away before it gets into the basement.

44 **Basement Floor Slab** - The 4- or 5-inch layer of concrete that forms the basement floor.

45 **Gravel Fill** - Placed under the slab to allow drainage and to guard against a damp floor.

46 **Girder** - A main beam upon which floor joists rest. Usually of steel, but also of wood.

47 **Backfill** - Earth, once dug out, that has been replaced and tamped down around the foundation.

48 **Areaway** - An open space to allow light and air to a window. Also called a light well.

49 **Area Wall** - The wall, of metal or concrete, that forms the open area.

E **Windows and Doors**

50 **Window** - An opening in a building for admitting light and air. It usually has a pane or panes of glass and is set in a frame or sash that is generally movable for opening and shutting.

51 **Window Frame** - The lining of the window opening.

52 **Window Sash** - The inner frame, usually movable, that holds the glass.

53 **Lintel** - The structural beam over a window or door opening.

54 **Window Casing** - The decorative strips surrounding a window opening on the inside.

F Stairs and Entry

55 **Entrance Canopy** - A roof extending over the entrance door.

56 **Furring** - Falsework or framework necessary to bring the outer surface to where we want it.

57 **Stair Tread** - The horizontal strip where we put our foot when we climb up or down the stairs.

58 **Stair Riser** - The vertical board connecting one tread to the next.

59 **Stair Stringer** - The sloping board that supports the ends of the steps.

60 **Newel** - The post that terminates the railing.

61 **Stair Rail** - The bar used for a handhold when we use the stairs.

62 **Balusters** - Vertical rods or spindles supporting a rail.

III. Structure

A Foundation

The word **foundation** is used to mean:
1. Construction below grade such as footings, cellar or basement walls.
2. The composition of the earth on which the building rests.
3. Special construction such as pilings and piers used to support the building.

The foundation bed may be composed of solid rock, sand, gravel, or unconsolidated sand or clay. Rock, sand, or gravel are the most reliable foundation materials. Unconsolidated sand and clay, though found in many sections of the country, are not as desirable, because they are subject to sliding and settling.

The footing (see Figure 2) distributes the weight of the building over a sufficient area of ground so as to ensure that the foundation walls will stand properly. Footings are usually constructed of a masonry-type material such as concrete; however, in the past wood and stone have been used. Some older houses have been constructed without footings.

Although it is usually difficult to determine the condition of a footing without excavating the foundation, a footing in a state of disrepair or lack of a footing will usually be indicated either by large

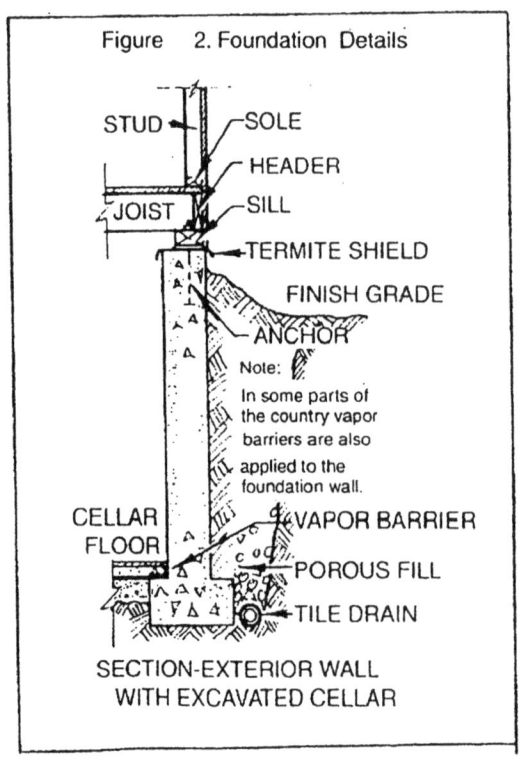

Figure 2. Foundation Details

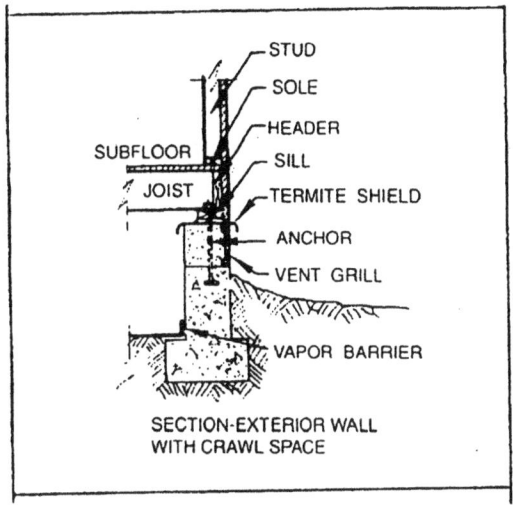

SECTION-EXTERIOR WALL WITH CRAWL SPACE

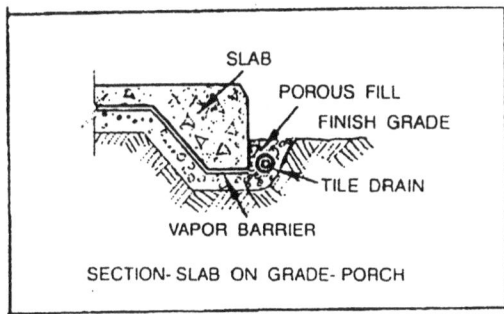

SECTION- SLAB ON GRADE- PORCH

cracks or by settlement in the foundation walls (see Figure 3).

Foundation wall cracks are usually diagonal, starting from the top, the bottom; or the end of the wall. Cracks that do not extend to at least one edge of the wall may not be caused by foundation problems. Such wall cracks may be due to other structural problems and should also be reported.

The foundation walls support the weight of the structure and transfer this weight to the footings. The foundation walls may be made of stone, brick, concrete, or concrete blocks and should be moisture proofed with either a membrane of water-proof material or a coating of portland cement mortar. The membrane may consist of plastic sheeting or a sandwich of standard roofing felt joined and covered with tar or asphalt. The purpose of waterproofing the foundation walls is to prevent water from penetrating the wall material and leaving the basement or cellar walls damp.

Holes in the foundation walls are a common finding in many old houses. These holes may be caused by missing bricks or blocks. Holes and cracks in a foundation wall are undesirable because they make a convenient entry for rats and other rodents and also indicate the possibility of further structural deterioration. These holes should not be confused with adequately installed vents in the foundation wall that permit ventilation and prevent moisture entrapment.

The basement or cellar floor should be made of concrete placed on at least 6 inches of gravel. The purpose of a concrete floor is to protect the basement or cellar from invasion by rodents or from flooding. The gravel distributes ground water movements under the concrete floor, reducing the possibility of the water's penetrating the floor. A waterproof membrane, such as plastic sheeting, should be laid before the concrete is placed for additional protection against flooding.

The basement or cellar floor should be gradually but uniformly sloped towards a drain or a series of drains from all directions. These drains permit the basement or cellar floor to be drained if it becomes flooded.

Evidence of ineffective waterproofing or moisture proofing will be indicated by water or moisture marks on the floor and walls.

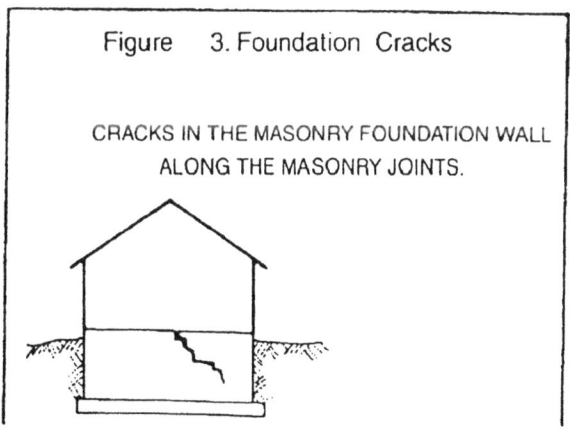

Figure 3. Foundation Cracks

CRACKS IN THE MASONRY FOUNDATION WALL ALONG THE MASONRY JOINTS.

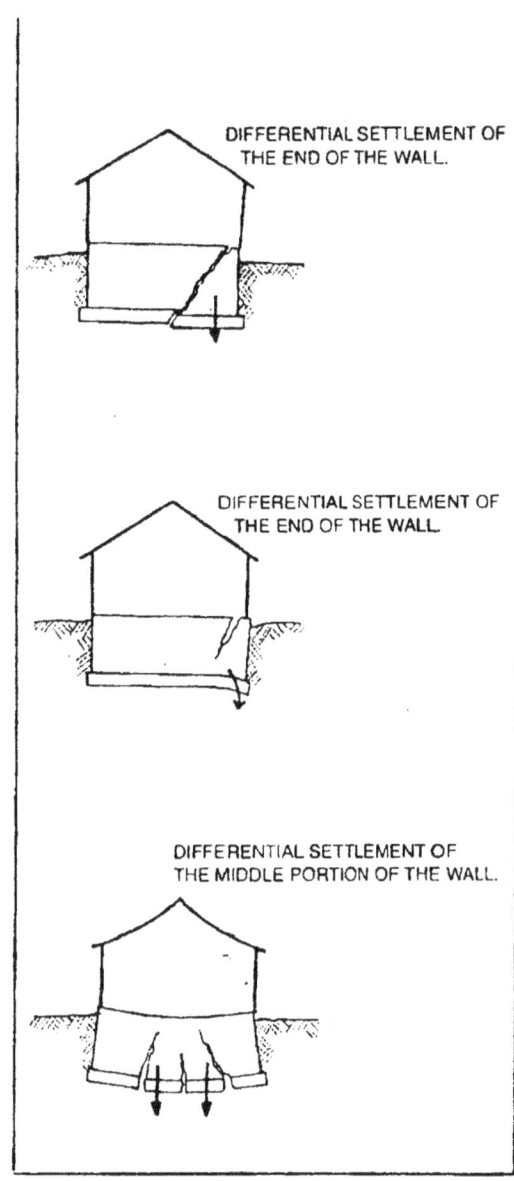

DIFFERENTIAL SETTLEMENT OF THE END OF THE WALL.

DIFFERENTIAL SETTLEMENT OF THE END OF THE WALL.

DIFFERENTIAL SETTLEMENT OF THE MIDDLE PORTION OF THE WALL.

Cellar doors, hatchways, and basement windows should be weathertight and rodent proof. A hatchway can be inspected by standing at the lower portion with the doors closed; if daylight can be seen, the door probably needs repair.

B Framing

Many different types of house-framing systems are found in various sections of the country; however, the majority of the members in each framing system are the same. They include:

1 **Foundation Sills:** (see Figure 4 and 5). The purpose of the sill is to provide support or a bearing surface for the outside walls of the building. The sill is the first part of the frame to be placed and rests directly on the foundation wall. It is bolted to the foundation wall by sill anchors. It is good practice to protect the sill against termites by extending the foundation wall to at least 18 inches above the ground and using a non-corroding metal shield continuously around the outside top of the foundation wall.

2 **Flooring Systems:** (see Figure 5). The flooring system is composed of a combination of girders, joists, sub-flooring, and finished flooring that may be made up of concrete, steel, or wood. Joists are laid perpendicular to the girders, at about 16 inches on centers, and are the members to which the sub-flooring is attached. When the subfloor is wood, it may be nailed at either right angles or diagonally to the joists.

As shown in Figure 5, a girder is a member that in certain framing systems supports the joists and is usually a larger section than the joists it supports. Girders are found in framing systems where there are no interior bearing walls or where the span between bearing walls is greater than the joists are capable of spanning. The most common application of a girder is to support the first floor in residences. Often a board known as a ledger is applied to the side of a wood girder or beam to form a ledge for the joists to rest upon. The girder, in turn, is supported by wood posts or steel "lally columns" which extend from the cellar or basement floor to the girder.

3 **Studs:** (see Figure 4 and 5). Wall studs are almost always 2 by 4

inches; studs 2 by 6 inches are occasionally used to provide a wall thick enough to permit the passage of waste pipes. There are two types of walls or partitions: bearing and non-bearing. A bearing wall is constructed at right angles to and supports the joists. A nonbearing wall or partition acts as a screen or enclosure; hence, the headers in it are often parallel to the joists of the floor above.

In general, studs like joists are spaced 16 inches on center. In light construction such as garages and summer cottages where plaster is omitted, or some other material is used for a wall finish, wider spacing on studs is common.

Openings for windows or doors must be framed in studs. This framing consists of horizontal members called "headers," and vertical members called "trimmers" (see Figure 1).

Since the vertical spaces between studs can act as flues to transmit flames in the event of a fire, "fire stops" are important in preventing or retarding fire from spreading through a building by way of air passages in walls, floors, and partitions. Fire stops are wood obstructions placed between studs or floor joists to prevent fire from spreading in these natural fluespaces.

4 **Interior Wall Finish:** Many types of materials are used for covering interior walls and ceilings, but the principal types are plaster and dry-wall construction. Plaster is a mixture, usually lime, sand, and water, applied in two or three coats to lath to form a hard-wall surface. Dry-wall finish is a material that requires little, if any, water for application. More specifically, dry-wall finish may be gypsum board, plywood, fiberboard, or wood in various sizes and forms.

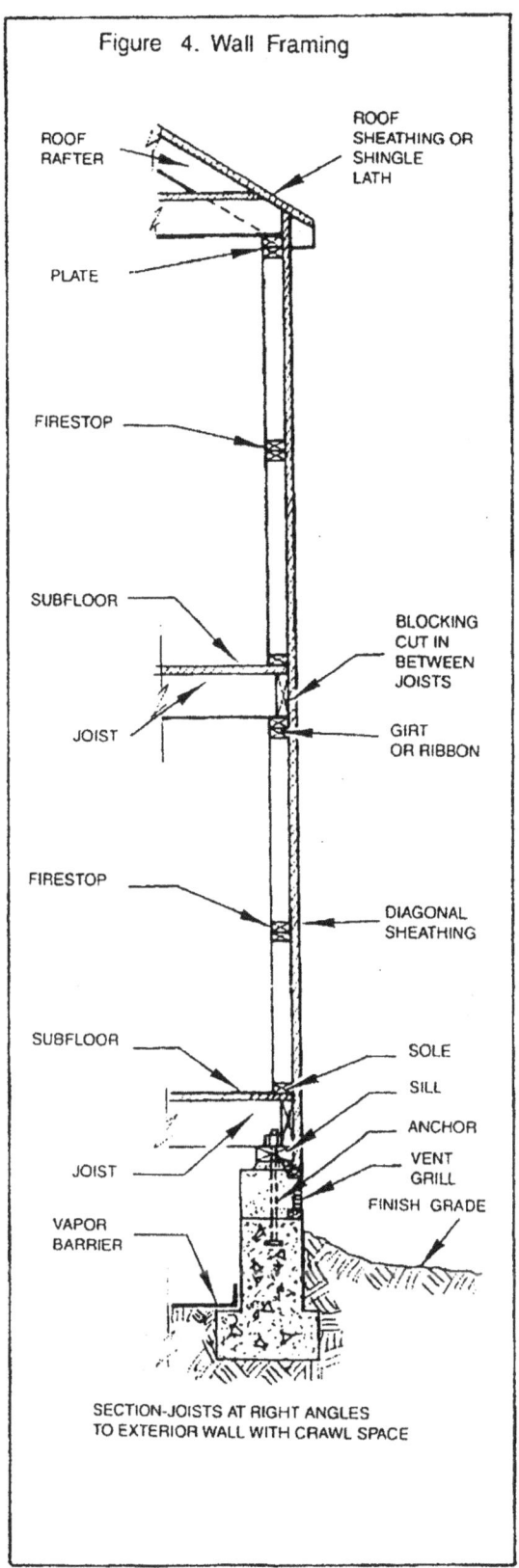

Figure 4. Wall Framing

SECTION-JOISTS AT RIGHT ANGLES TO EXTERIOR WALL WITH CRAWL SPACE

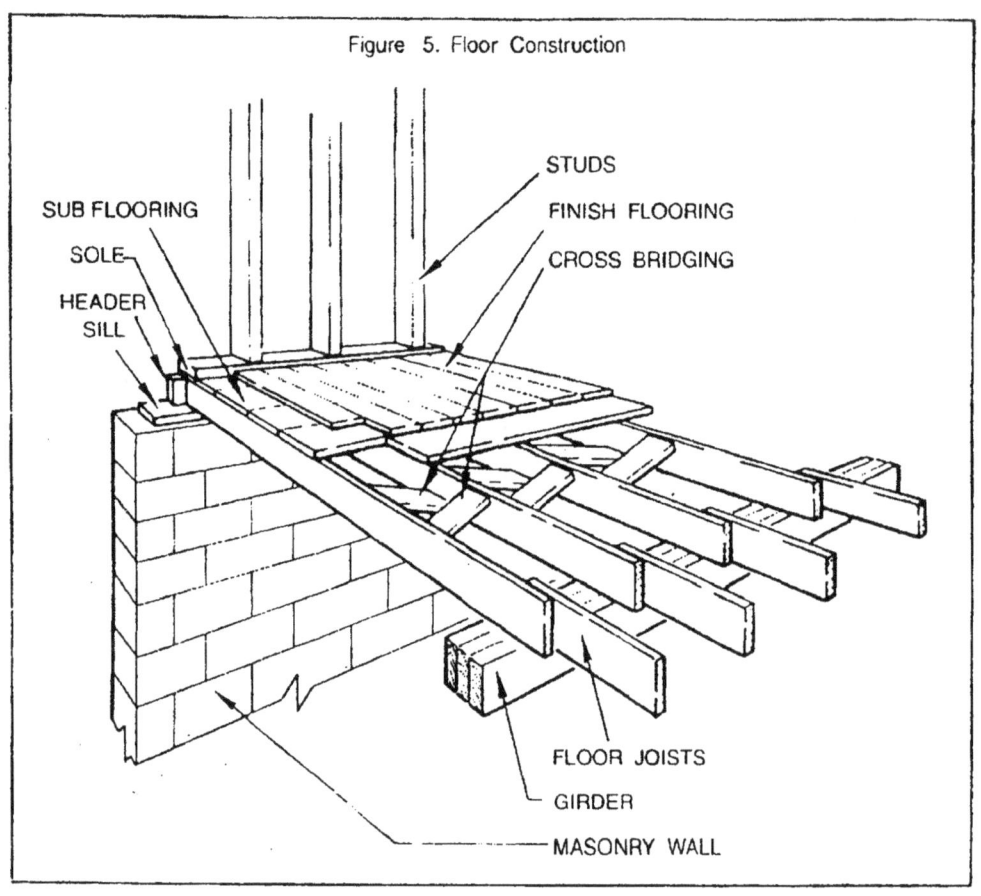

Figure 5. Floor Construction

Gypsum board is a sheet material composed of a gypsum filler faced with paper. Sheets are usually 4 feet wide and can be obtained in lengths up to 12 feet. In dry-wall construction, gypsum boards are fastened to the studs either vertically or horizontally and then painted. The edges along the length of the sheet are recessed to receive joint cement and tape.

A plaster finish requires a base upon which plaster can be spread. Wood lath at one time was the plaster base most commonly used, but today gypsum-board lath is more popular. It has paper faces with a gypsum filler. Such lath is 16 by 48 inches and 1/2 or 3/8 inches thick.

It is applied horizontally across the studs. Gypsum lath may be perforated to improve the bond and thus lengthen the time the plaster can remain intact when exposed to fire. The building codes in some cities require that gypsum lath be perforated. Expanded-metal lath may also be used as a plaster base. Expanded-metal lath consists of sheet metal slit and expanded to form openings to hold the plaster. Metal lath is usually 27 by 96 inches and is fastened to the studs.

Plaster is applied over the base to a minimum thickness of 1/2 inch. Because some drying may take place in wood-framing members after the house is completed, some shrinkage can be expected, which, in turn, may cause plaster cracks to develop around openings and in corners. Strips of lath imbedded in the plaster at these locations prevent cracks.

On the inside face of studs that form an exterior wall, vapor barriers are used to prevent condensation on the wall. The vapor barrier is an asphalted paper or metal foil through which moisture-laden air cannot travel.

5. **Stairways:** (see Figure 6). The general purpose of the standards for stairway dimensions is to ensure that there is adequate headroom, width, and uniformity in riser and tread size of every step to accommodate the expected traffic on each stairway safely.

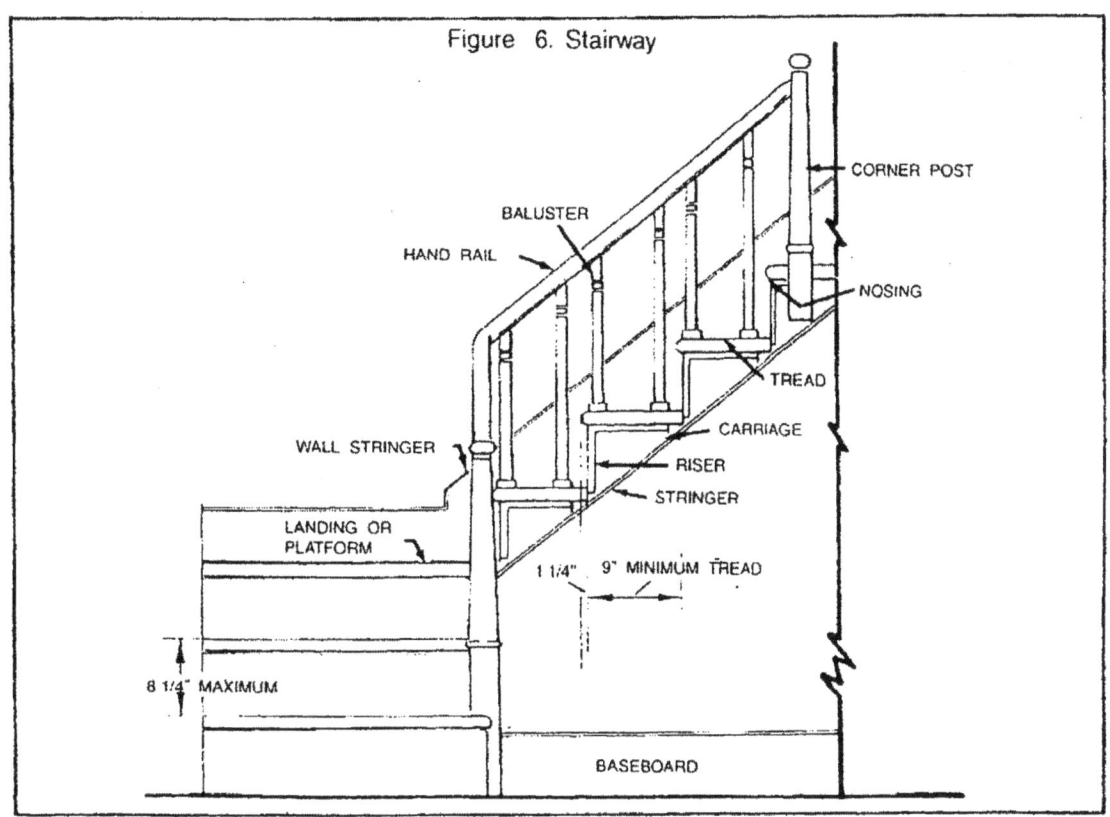

Figure 6. Stairway

Interior stairways should be not less than 44 inches in width. The width of a stairway may be reduced to 36 inches in one- and two-family dwellings. Stairs with closed risers should have maximum risers of 8 1/4 inches and a minimum tread of 9 inches plus 1 1/4-inch nosing. Basement stairs are often constructed with open risers. These stairs should have maximum risers of 8 1/4 inches and minimum treads of 9 inches plus 1/2-inch nosing. The headroom in all parts of the stair enclosure should be no less than 80 inches.

Exterior stairway dimensions should be the same as those called for in interior stairways, except that the headroom requirement does not apply.

6. **Windows:** The four general classifications of windows for residences are:

10

a Double-hung sash window that moves up or down, balanced by weights hung on chains or ropes, or springs on each side.

b Casement window sash is hinged at the side and can be hung so that it will swing outward or inward.

c Awning window - usually has two or more glass panes that are hinged at the top and swing about a horizontal axis.

d Sliding window - usually has two or more glass panes that slide past one another on a horizontal track.

The principal parts of a double-hung window (see Figure 4-7) are the lights, the top rail-framing members, bars or muntins that separate the lights, stiles - side-framing members, bottom rail, sash weights, and sash cords or chains. (All rails are horizontal, all stiles vertical.) The casement window's principal parts include: top and bottom rails, muntins, butt hinges, and jamb. All types of windows should open freely and close securely.

The exterior sill is the bottom projection of a window. The drip cap is a separate piece of wood projecting over the top of the window and is a component of the window casing.

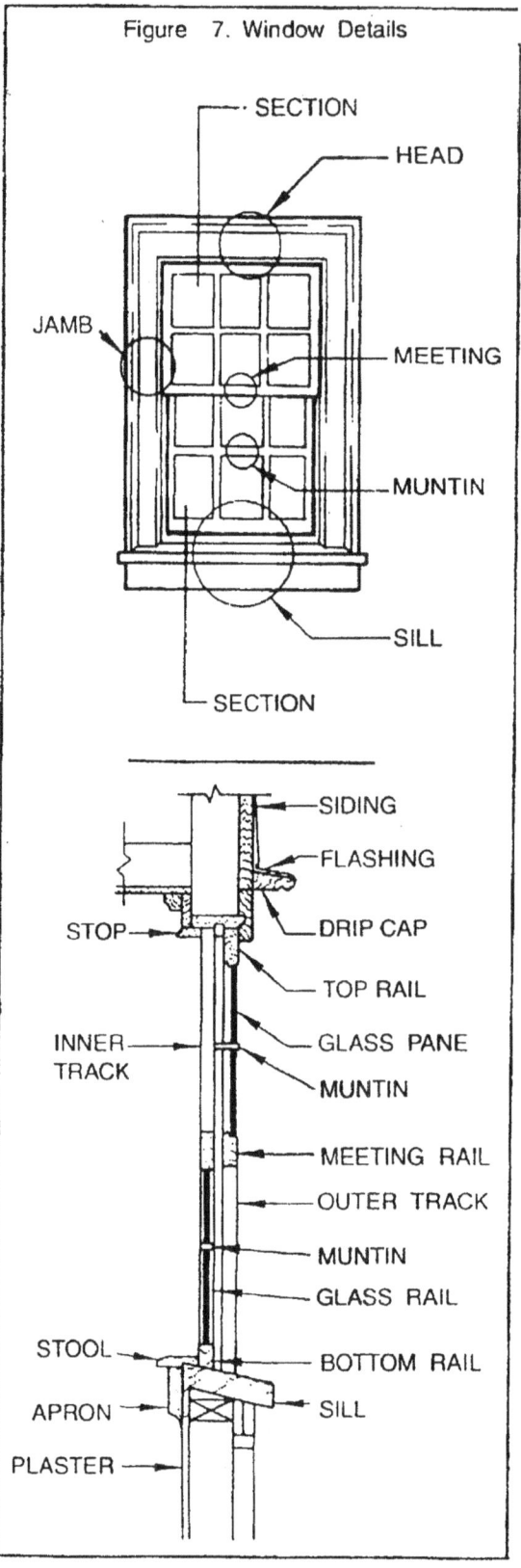

Figure 7. Window Details

7 **Doors:** There are many styles of doors both for exterior and interior use. Interior doors should offer a rea-

sonable degree of privacy. Exterior doors must, in addition to offering privacy, protect the interior of the structure from the elements. The various parts of a door have the same definitions as the corresponding parts of a window.

The most common types of doors are:

a **Batten door**: This consists of boards nailed together in various ways. The simplest is two layers nailed to each other at right angles, usually with each layer at 45 degrees to the vertical.

Another type of batten door consists of vertical boards nailed at right angles to several (two to four) cross strips called ledgers, with diagonal bracing members nailed between ledgers. If vertical members corresponding to ledgers are added at the sides, the verticals are called frames.

Batten doors are often found in cellars and other places where appearance is not a factor and economy is desired.

b **Flush doors**: Solid flush doors are perfectly flat, usually on both sides, although occasionally they are made flush on one side and paneled on the other. Flush doors sometimes are solid planking, but they are commonly veneered and possess a core of small pieces of white pine or other wood. These pieces are glued together with staggered end joints. Along the sides, top, and bottom are glued 3/4-inch edge strips of the same wood, used to create a smooth surface that can be cut or planed. The front and back faces are then covered with a 1/8-to 1/4-inch layer of veneer.

Solid flush doors may be used on both the interior and exterior.

c **Hollow-core doors**: These, like solid flush doors, are perfectly flat, but unlike solid doors, the core consists mainly of a grid of crossed wooden slats or some other type of grid construction. Faces are 3-ply plywood instead of one or two plies of veneer, and the surface veneer may be any species of wood, usually hardwood. The edges of the core are solid wood and are made wide enough at the appropriate places to accommodate locks and butts. Doors of this kind are considerably lighter than solid flush doors.

Hollow-core doors are usually used as interior doors.

d **Paneled doors**: Most doors are paneled, with most panels consisting of solid wood or plywood, either "raised" or "flat," although exterior doors frequently have one or more panels of glass, in which case they are called "lights." One or more panels may be employed although the number seldom exceeds eight. Paneled doors may be used both on the interior or exterior.

In addition to the various types of wood doors, metal is often used as a veneer or for the frame.

In general, the horizontal members are called rails and the vertical members are called stiles. Every door has a top and bottom rail, and some may have intermediate rails. There are always at least two stiles, one on each side of the door. The frame of a doorway is the portion to which the door is hinged. It consists of two side jambs and a head jamb, with an integral or attached stop against which the door closes.

Exterior door frames are ordinarily of softwood plank, with side rabbitted to receive the door in the same way as casement windows. At the foot is a sill, made of hardwood to withstand the wear of traffic, and sloped down and out to shed water.

Interior door frames are similar to exterior, except that they are often set directly on the hardwood flooring without a sill.

Building codes throughout the country call for doors in various locations within the structure to be fire resistant. These doors are often covered with metal or some other fire-resistant materials, and some are completely constructed of metal. Fire-resistant doors are usually located between a garage and a house, stairwells and hallways, all boiler rooms. The fire resistance rating required for various doors differs with local fire codes

C **Roof Framing** (see Figures 1, 4, 8, and 9)

Rafters serve the same purpose for the roof as joists do for floors, i.e., providing support for sheathing and roofing material. Rafters are usually spaced 20 inches on center.

1. **Collar Beam:** Collar beams are ties between rafters on opposite sides of the roof. If the attic is to be used for rooms, the collar beam may double as the ceiling joist.

2. **Purlin:** A purlin is the horizontal member that forms the support for the rafters at the intersection of the two slopes of a gambrel roof.

3. **Ridge Board:** A ridge board is a horizontal member against which the rafters rest at their upper ends; it forms a lateral tie to make them secure.

4. **Hip:** Like a ridge except that it slopes. The intersection of two adjacent, rather than two opposite, roof planes.

5. **Roof Boards:** The manner in which roof boards are applied depends upon the type of roofing material. Roof boards may vary from tongue-and-groove lumber to plywood panels.

6. **Dormer:** The term dormer window is applied to all windows in the roof of a building, whatever their size and shape.

D **Exterior Walls and Trim** (see Figure 4 and 9)

Exterior walls are enclosure walls whose purpose is to make the building weathertight. In most one- to three-story buildings they also serve as bearing walls. These walls may be made of many different materials.

Frequently used framed exterior walls appear to be of brick construction. In this situation, the brick is only one course thick and is called a brick veneer. It supports nothing but itself and is kept from toppling by ties connected to the frame wall.

In frame construction the base material of the exterior walls is called "sheathing." The sheathing material may be square-edge, shiplap, or tongue-and-groove boards.

In recent construction there has been a strong trend toward the use of plywood or composition panels.

13

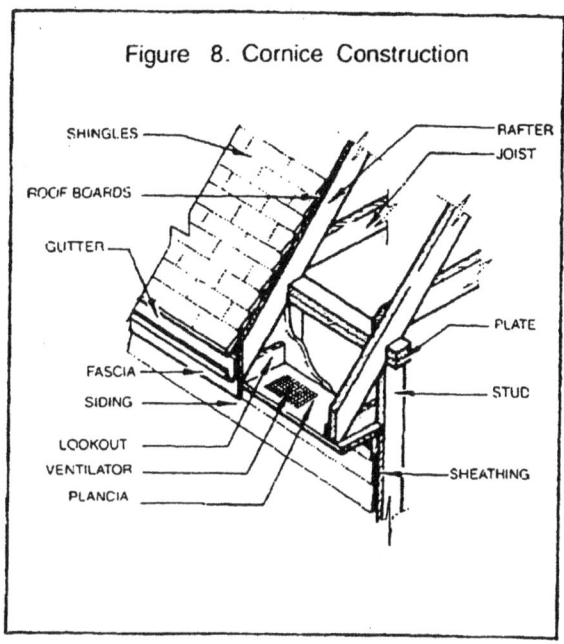

Figure 8. Cornice Construction

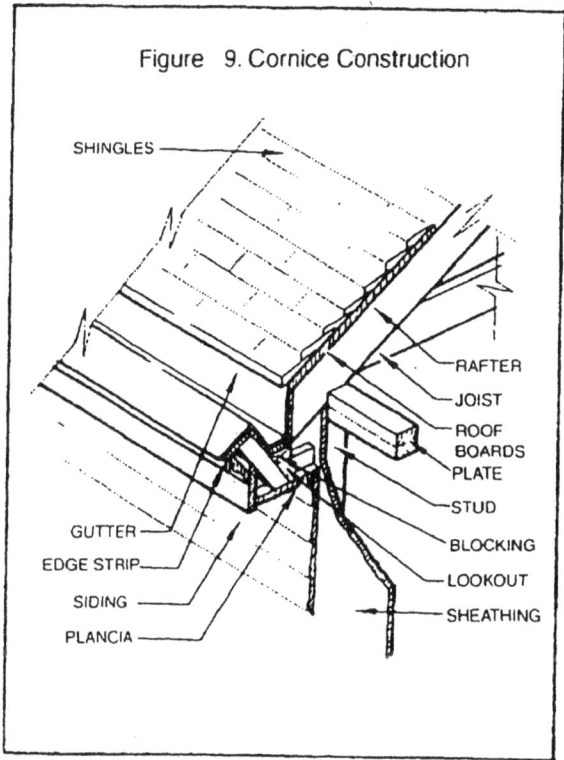

Figure 9. Cornice Construction

Sheathing, in addition to serving as a base course for the finished siding material, stiffens the frame to resist sway caused by wind. It is for this reason that sheathing has been applied diagonally on frame buildings.

The finished siding may be clapboard, shingles, aluminum, brick asphalt, wood, and so forth, or a combination thereof. Good aluminum siding has a backer board that serves as added insulation and affords rigidity to the siding. Projecting cornices are a decorative trim found at the top of the building's roofline. A parapet wall is that part of the masonry wall that extends up and beyond the roofline and is capped with a noncombustible material. It helps prevent spread of fire, provides a rest for fire department ladders, and helps prevent people on the roof from falling off.

Many types of siding, shingles, and other exterior coverings are applied over the sheathing. Wood siding, cedar, and other wood shingles or shakes, clapboard, common siding (called bevel siding), composition siding, asbestos, cement shingles, asbestos-cement siding, and the aforementioned aluminum siding are commonly used for exterior coverings. Clapboards and common siding differ only in the length of the pieces. Clapboards are 4 feet long while panel siding comes in lengths from 6 to 16 feet. Composition siding is made of felt and asphalt, which are often shaped to look like brick. Asbestos and cement shingles are rigid and produce a covering that is fire resistant. Cedar wood shingles are also manufactured with a backer board that gives insulation and fire-resistant qualities. Asbestos cement siding made of asbestos fiber and portland cement has good fire-resistant qualities and is a rigid covering.

E Roof Coverings (Flexible Material Class)

1 **Asphalt Shingle:** The principal damage to asphalt shingle roofs is caused by the action of strong winds on shingles nailed too high. Usually the shingles affected by winds are those in the four or five courses nearest the ridge and in the area

111

extending about 5 feet down from the edge or rake of the roof.

2. **Asphalt Built-up Roofs:** These may be un-surfaced, the coating of bitumen being exposed directly to the weather, or they may be surfaced having slag or gravel imbedded in the bituminous coating. The use of surfacing material is desirable as a protection against wind damage and the elements. This type of roof should have enough pitch to drain water readily.

3. **Coal Tar Pitch Built-up Roofs:** This type roof must be surfaced with slag or gravel. Coal tar pitch built-up roof should always be used on deck pitched less than 1/2 inch per foot; that is, where waler may collect and stand. This type roof should be inspected on completion, 6 months later, and then at least once a year, preferably in the fall. When the top coating of bitumen shows damage or has become badly weathered, it should be renewed (rigid material class).

4. **Slate Roofs:** The most common problem with slate roofs is the replacement of broken slates. Roofs of this type normally render long service with little or no repair.

5. **Tile Roofs:** Replacement of broken shingle tiles is the main maintenance problem. This is one of the most expensive roofing materials. It requires very little maintenance and gives long service.

6. **Copper Roofs:** Usually are of 16-ounce copper sheeting and applied to permanent structures. When properly installed, they require practically no maintenance or repair. Proper installation allows for expansion and contraction with changes in temperature.

7. **Galvanized Iron Roofs:** Maintenance is done principally by removing rust and keeping roof well painted. Leaks can be corrected by re-nailing, caulking, or replacing all or part of the sheet or sheets in disrepair.

8. **Wood Shingle Roofs:** The most important factors of this type roof are its pitch and exposure, the character of wood, kind of nails used, and preservative treatment given shingles. Creosote and coal tar preservative are satisfactory for both treated and untreated shingles.

9. **Flashing:** Valleys in roofs that are formed by the junction of two downward slopes may be finished, open, or closed. In a closed valley the slates, tiles, or shingles of one side meet those of the other, and the flashing below them may be comparatively narrow. In an open valley, the flashing, which may be made of zinc, copper, or aluminum, is laid in a continuous strip, extending 12 to 18 inches on each side of the valley, while the tiles or slates do not come within 4 to 6 inches of it.

   The ridges built up on a sloping roof where it runs down against a vertical projection, like a chimney or a skylight, should be weather-proofed with flashing.

   Metal flashings are generally used with slate, tile, metal, and wood shingles. Failure of roof flashing is usually due to exposed nails that have come loose. The loose nails allow the flashing to lift with leakage resulting.

10. **Gutters and Leaders:** Gutters and leaders should be of noncombustible materials. They should be securely fastened to the structure and spill into a storm sewer if the neighborhood is so provided. When there is no storm sewer, a concrete or stone block placed on the ground beneath the leader prevents water from eroding the lawn. This store

block is called a splash block. Gutters will not become plugged if protected against clogging of leaves and twigs. Gutters should be checked every spring and fall and then cleaned out when necessary.

IV. Discussion of Inspection Techniques

A serious building defect may often be observed during a housing inspector's routine examination. In many cases it is beyond the scope of the housing inspector's background to analyze the underlying causes and to recommend a course of action that will facilitate repair in an efficient and economical manner. In situations such as this, it is important that the inspector realize his limitations and refer the matter to the proper expert.

A prime example of a technically complex situation that a housing inspector might observe is a leaning, buckling, or bulging foundation or bearing wall. This problem may be the result of a number of hidden or interacting problems. For example, it may be the result of differential building settlement or failure of a structural beam or girder. It is beyond the scope of the housing inspector's responsibilities to discover the cause of the defect, but it is his responsibility to note the problem and refer it to the proper authority. In this case the proper authority would be a building inspector.

In the aforementioned situation where a bulging foundation wall was discovered, this would obviously constitute a violation of the housing ordinance and should be written up as such by the housing inspector. Since the housing inspector is generally not qualified to determine whether the house should be evacuated because it is in danger of imminent collapse, he should seek the advice of a building inspector.

A question that frequently arises is *which violations should be referred to an expert?* Needless to say, circumstances that obviously fall within the jurisdiction of another department should be referred to the department. The housing inspector should discuss with his supervisor any situation in which he feels inadequate to make a decision. In all cases the inspector should inform his supervisor before referring a problem to another agency or expert.

Another reason for referral to other departments is that when a remedial action is completed the other department will be in a better position to determine whether the job is satisfactory.

This principle of referral should be applied to every portion of the inspection, whether it deals with health, heating, plumbing, gas, or electrical as well as structural defects.

Certain structural items should be recognized as unsafe by the housing inspector. For example, a beam that has sagged or slanted may cause a portion of or an entire floor to sag or slope. Where a sagging or sloping floor is found, examine the ceiling of the room below or the basement for a broken or dropped girder or joist.

Doors and windows that are out of level will not close completely. It may be possible to see outside light through openings around window rails and door jambs. If an inspector detects such a situation, the condition of the supporting girders, girts, posts, and studs should be questioned, since this condition is evidence that some of these members may be termite infested or rotted and may be causing the outside wall to sag. Glass panes in doors and windows should be replaced if found to be broken or missing. Windows should also be checked for proper operation, and items such as broken sash cords or chains noted.

If the roof of the structure appears to be sagging, the inspector should make a special effort to examine the rafters, purlin, collar beams, and ridge boards if these members are exposed as in unfinished attics. The condition of the roof boards may be examined while he is in the attic. If light can be seen between these boards the roof is unsound. Evidence of a leaking roof will be indicated by loose plaster or peeling or stained paint and wall paper. Areas of the roof where flashing occurs, such as around the chimney, are frequent origins of roof leaks. It is essential that the leak be found and repaired, not only to prevent the entrance of moisture into the building, but also to prevent the loosening of the plaster, rotting of timbers, and extension of damage to the remainder of the house.

Gutters and rain leaders should be placed around the entire building to insure proper drainage of water. This will lessen the possibility of seepage of water through siding and window frames, and entrance of water into the cellar or basement. Lack of or leaking gutters may result in rotting of the siding or erosion of the exposed portion of the cellar or basement walls. This situation commonly exists where the mortar between bricks or concrete blocks in foundation walls is found to be heavily eroded. Gutters should be free from dirt and leaves.

The exterior siding should be in sound, weathertight condition. Peeled or worn paint on wood siding will expose the bare wood to the elements and result in splitting and warping of siding. This condition will eventually lead to the entrance of rain water with resultant rotting of the sheathing and studs as well as inside dampness and falling plaster. Sound and painted siding will prevent major repairs and expenses in the future. This condition will often be particularly prevalent on the north face of the structure.

Roof and chimneys should be inspected for tilting, missing bricks, deterioration of flashing, and pointing of chimney bricks. In addition, roof covering should be checked for broken spots and missing shingles or tiles. Roof doors should be metal clad, self-closing, tight fitting, and unlockable. The roof should also be examined for weather-tightness and broken TV antennas.

Porches should be carefully examined for weakened treads, missing or cracked boards, holes, and holes covered with tin plates, railing rigidity, missing posts, handrail rigidity, condition of the columns that support the porch roof, and the condition of the porch roof itself. The open section beneath the porch should be inspected for broken lattice-work. Check under the porch for accumulation of dirt and debris that can offer a harborage for vermin and rodents.

Loose plaster and missing or peeling wallpaper or paint should be noted. Bugs and cockroaches eat the paste from the wallpaper while leaving behind loose paper.

The basic parts of a stairway that a housing inspector should be able to identify correctly are the following:

A Riser

B Tread

C Nosing

D Handrail

E Balustrade and Balusters, the Vertical Members that Support the Handrail, and

F The Soffit, Underpart of the Stairway.

In the examination of a stairway (be careful to turn the light on) initially check the underside, if visible, to see if it is intact. Then proceed slowly up the stairs placing full weight on each tread and checking for loose, wobbling, or uneven treads and risers. Regardless of the size of the treads or risers they should all be of uniform size. For all stairs that rise 3 or more feet, a handrail should be present and in a sound and rigid condition.

Any fireplace should conform to the requirements of the local code. An unused fireplace that has its opening covered with wallpaper or other material should have a solid seal behind the paper. Operable fireplaces should have a workable damper and a fire screen, and should be clean.

Garages and accessory structures should be inspected in the same manner as the main building.

Sidewalks and driveways, whether constructed of flagstone, concrete, or asphalt, should be checked for creaking, buckling, and other conditions dangerous to pedestrian travel.

Stone, brick, or concrete steps should be inspected for cracks, deterioration, and pointing.

Fences should be in a sound condition and painted. Fire escapes should be checked for paint condition, loose or broken treads and rails, proper operating condition, and proper connection to the house.

V. Noise as an Environmental Stress

People feel comfortable in an environment with a low-level, soothing, steady, unobstrusive level of sound, typical of the natural undisturbed environment. All of us have experienced the anguish that noise can cause, whether it be noise from a neighbor's television, the grinding of truck gears while asleep, the persistent whine of a fan motor, or the sound of children racing down the halls. These annoyances experienced in the home are producing public demands for noise control legislation.

Not only is noise disturbing, but studies also indicate that extreme noise can cause deafness and perhaps interfere with other bodily functions.

While few existing housing ordinances contain enforceable noise provisions, noise problems must be considered by the building inspector because they intimately affect and are affected by his decisions. As a housing inspector, you can help residents by suggesting corrective noise measures that can be taken; you can refer them to agencies, if needed, for corrective action; you can help them to understand that their noisy environment can place limitations on their behavior, capabilities, and satisfaction with their home.

Noise is unwanted sound. Noise can travel through air or through the building structure. The first stage of noise control is the control of sound at its source. If attempts to quiet the source are not completely successful, then other, more expensive corrective measures will be required.

Although a visual examination of a dwelling may detect some sources of noise leaks (see Figure 10) such as wide gaps or cracks at ceiling, floor, or adjoining wall edges, it is usually inadequate since it fails to detect sources of noise leaks hidden from the eye. A far more effective test is to be alert for the operation of some noisy device like a vacuum cleaner in a closed room and listen near the other side of the wall for any noise leakage. The ear is a reasonably good sensing device. If a noise leak is noticed, the partition may be surveyed at critical points with a bright flashlight while an observer looks for light leakage in a darkened room on the other side. Detection of any light leakage in the darkened room will signify a noise leak.

Noise carried as vibration by a building structure is called structure-borne noise. Detecting structure-borne noise caused by the operation of mechanical equipment is somewhat more difficult (see Figure 11). With noisy equipment in operation, the inspector can sometimes locate noise leaks or structure-borne noise paths by conducting similar hearing tests along with pressing the ear against various room surfaces or using fingertips to sense the vibration of these surfaces.

A Airborne Noise

The sources of airborne noise that cause the most frequent disturbances in the home are audio instruments such as televisions, radios, phonographs, or pianos; adults and children speaking loudly, singing, crying and shouting; household appliances such as garbage disposals, dishwashers, vacuum cleaners, clothes washers, and dryers; plumbing noises such as pipes knocking, toilets flushing, and water running.

The disturbing influences of airborne noise are generally limited to the areas near the noise source. For example, a phonograph may cause annoyance in rooms of a neighbor's apartment adjacent to the phonograph but rarely in rooms farther removed unless doors or passageways are left open. Sound absorption materials such as carpeting, acoustical tile, drapery, and upholstered furniture in the intervening rooms may often provide a significant reduction in the disturbing noise before it reaches rooms where quiet is desired.

Under no conditions should sound-absorptive materials be used on the surfaces of walls and ceilings for the sole purpose of preventing the transmission of sound as structureborne noise. To do so would be a complete waste of effort. To illustrate, imagine the noise conducted by a wall constructed solely of drapery or acoustical tile attached to studs. The noise level in the room would be reduced, but sound produced in the room would pass through the wall to adjoining rooms with little, if any, reduction in noise level. Sound absorptive materials should be used in and near areas of high noise levels to limit airborne noise at the source of the noise and reduce the effects of noise along corridors.

The transmission of noise from one completely enclosed room to an adjoining room separated by a partition wall may be either direct transmission through the wall, indirect transmission through other walls, ceilings, and floors common to both rooms, or through corridors adjacent to such rooms.

In some older wood frame houses, the open troughs between studs and joists are efficient sound transmission paths. This noise transmission by indirect paths is known as "flanking transmission" (see Figure 10 and 11). In addition to the flanking paths, there may be noise leaks particularly along the ceiling, floor, and sidewall edges of the wall. In order to obtain the highest sound insulation performance, a partition wall must be of airtight construction. Care must be exercised to seal all openings, gaps, holes, joints, and penetrations of piping and conduits with a nonsetting caulking compound. Even hairline cracks, particularly at adjoining wall, floor, and ceiling edges, transmit a substantially greater amount of noise than would normally be expected on the basis of the size of the crack.

Figure 10. Flanking Transmission of Airborne Noise

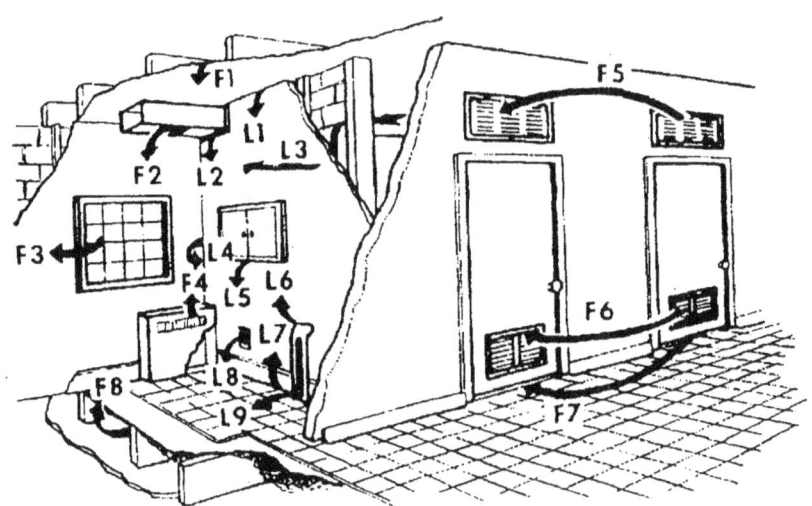

FLANKING NOISE PATHS	NOISE LEAKS
F1 Open plenums over walls, false ceilings	L1 Poor seal at ceiling edges
F2 Unbaffled duct runs	L2 Poor seal around duct penetrations
F3 Outdoor path, window to window	L3 Poor mortar joints, porous masonry block
F4 Continuous unbaffled inductor Units	L4 Poor seal at sidewall, filler panel, etc.
F5 Hall path, open vents	L5 Back-to-back cabinets, poor workmanship
F6 Hall path, louvered doors	L6 Holes, gaps at wall penetrations
F7 Hall path, openings under doors	L7 Poor seal at floor edges
F8 Open troughs in floor-ceiling structure	L8 Back-to-back electrical outlets
	L9 Holes, gaps at floor penetrations

Other points to consider are these: leaks are (a) batten strip A/O post connections of prefabricated walls, (b) under-floor pipe or service chases, (c) recessed, spanning light fixtures, (d) ceiling and floor cover plates of movable walls, (e) unsupported A/O unbacked wall-board joints (f) edges and backing of built-in cabinets and appliances, (g) prefabricated, hollow metal, exterior curtain walls.

It is often helpful to use one sound to drown out another disturbing noise; for example, music on the radio can be used to drown out the noise of traffic. The use of sound to drown out noise is particularly useful in masking noises that occur infrequently, such as accelerating or braking vehicles, periodic mechanical equipment noise, barking dogs, laughter, or shouting.

B **Structure-Borne Noise**

Structure-borne noise occurs when wall, floor, or other building elements are set into vibration by direct contact with vibrating sources such as mechanical equipment or domestic appliances. A small, vibrating pipe firmly attached to a plywood or gypsum wall panel will amplify the vibration noise. An illustration of this amplification of structure-borne noise is provided by the sound board of a piano. The major sources of structure-borne noise are the impact of walking on wood floors or of slamming doors, plumbing system noises, heating and air-conditioning system noises, noise from mechanical equipment or appliances, and vibration from sources outside the building. If the vibration is severe enough, it may have adverse effects not only on the occupants of a building but also on the building structure. Household appliances such as refrigerators, washing machines, sewing machines, clothes dryers, televisions, and pianos should be vibration isolated from the floor by means of rubber mounts placed under them if disturbing structure-borne noise is to be avoided. Residents should also be cautioned against locating these noise sources along party walls and in particular against mounting these appliances and kitchen cabinets directly on party walls so that the walls act as sounding boards in adjoining apartments. Window air-conditioners should be completely vibration isolated from the surrounding window frame by rubber gaskets and padding. The importance of isolating a vibrating source from the structure in the control of equipment noise cannot be overemphasized.

Another source of disturbing structure-borne noise is squeaking of wood floors. Some squeaks can be eliminated by lubricating the tongues of wood floor boards with mineral oil applied sparingly to the openings between adjacent boards. Loose finish flooring may be securely fastened to subflooring by surface nailing into the

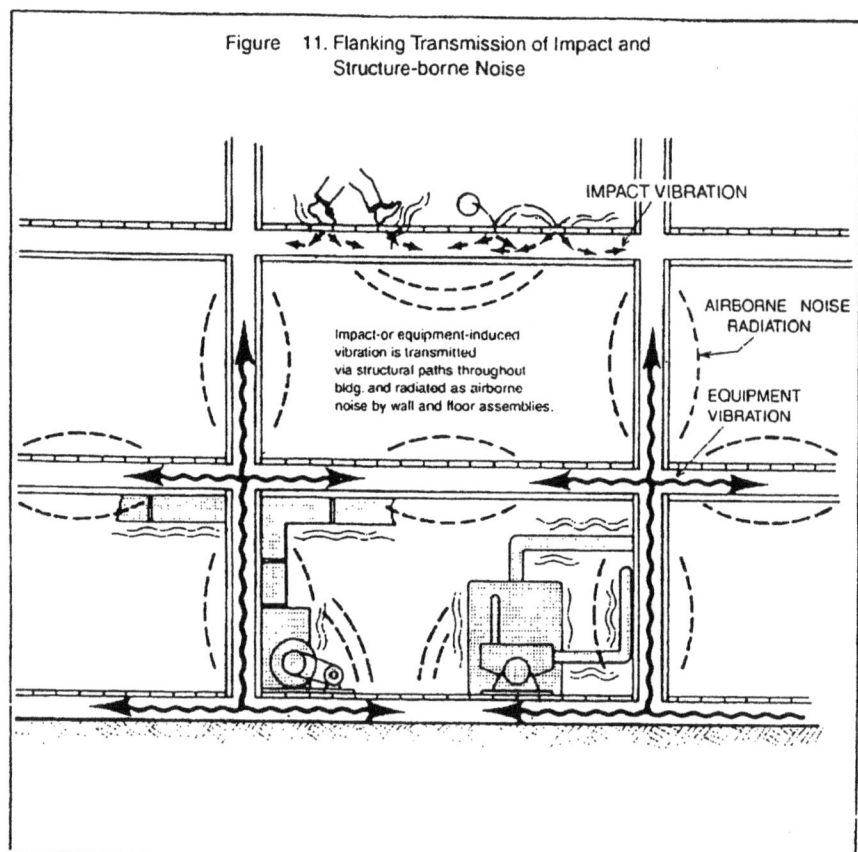

Figure 11. Flanking Transmission of Impact and Structure-borne Noise

subfloor and preferably the joists. Ring-type nails or sawtooth staples properly spaced should be used in nailing finish flooring to subflooring. In an exposed joist structure, where finish flooring is warped, driving screws up through the subfloor and into the finish floor will be effective in drawing the layers of flooring tightly together to reduce noise.

Of course, noise caused by the impact of walking or scraping can be substantially reduced by the use of carpets. In the case of door slams, the impact noise may be eliminated by the use of door closers or rubber bumpers.

The noisy hammering of a plumbing system is usually caused by the sudden interruption of water-flow, for example, by a quick closing or opening of a tap.

Air chambers can be built into the plumbing system to reduce water hammer. The air pockets, rubber inserts, or spring elements in air chambers act to reduce noise. Air chambers are explained in Chapter 6.

Defective, loose, or worn valve stems create intense chattering of the plumbing system. The defective device can frequently be found without difficulty, since immediate use of the device causes the vibration, which generally occurs at some low-flow-velocity setting and diminishes or disappears at a higher flow setting. For example, if a chattering noise occurs when a particular faucet or tap is opened partially and diminishes when fully opened, the faucet more than likely has some loose or defective parts and should be repaired.

Noise can be a very complex problem. The housing inspector is not expected to be an acoustics expert. Nor is he expected to be able to analyze and solve the noise problems that an acoustics consultant would normally handle. He can, however, help teach the public that the annoyances and stress caused by noise can be partially alleviated by a simple awareness of common noise problems found in many residences.

Although the housing inspector is not an expert in the fields of zoning, plumbing, building, and electrical systems, he should be familiar with the applicable code in each of the respective fields. Familiarization with these codes will better enable him to recognize violations.

ZONING ORDINANCES IN RELATION TO THE HOUSING INSPECTION

	Page
I. Background of Zoning	1
II. Definitions	2
III. Zoning Objectives	3
IV. What Zoning Cannot Do	4
V. Content of the Ordinance	4
VI. Bulk and Height requirements	5
VII. Yard Requirements	5
VIII. Off street Parking	6
IX. Nonconforming Uses	6
X. Variances	6
XI. Exceptions	7
XII. Administration	7
XIII. How Zoning Can Benefit the Housing Inspector	7
XIV. Example of Zoning and Housing Relationships	8

ZONING ORDINANCES IN RELATION TO THE HOUSING INSPECTION

Zoning is essentially a means of ensuring that a community's hind uses are compatibly located for the health, safety, and general welfare of the community. Experience has shown that some types of controls are needed in order to provide orderly growth in relation to the community plan for development. Just as a capital improvement program governs public improvements such as streets, parks, and other recreational facilities, schools, and public buildings, so zoning governs the planning program with respect to the use of public and private property.

When a person buys or builds a house or other structure in a municipality that has a zoning ordinance in effect, he is presumed to know and obliged by law to comply with the zoning regulations governing the use of buildings and land in the section of the community in which his property is located. If he either erects a structure or converts a house or building that is within that particular district by the local zoning ordinance into another type of use he still has acquired no property right to continue the forbidden use. An example would be the conversion of a single family residence into multifamily units. Even if the owner has obtained a building permit for this work already completed, the building permit would be voided, because the work was started in violation of the zoning code and because a building permit can be valid' only when issued for a lawful purpose. The building inspector is therefore obliged to refuse issuance of a building permit if the proposed work is in violation of the zoning ordinance.

It is very important that the housing inspector know the general nature of zoning regulations, since properties in violation of both the housing code and the zoning ordinance must be brought into full compliance with the zoning ordinance before the housing code can be enforced. In many cases the housing inspector may be able to eliminate some of the properties in violation of the housing code through enforcement of the zoning ordinance.

I. Background of Zoning

Zoning regulations have been used for several centuries. In the early settlement of our country, gunpowder mills and storehouses were prohibited from being located within the heavily populated portions of town, owing to the frequent fires and explosions. Later, zoning took the form of fire districts, and under implied legislative powers, wooden buildings were prohibited from certain sections of the municipality.

Massachusetts passed one of the first zoning laws in 1692. This law authorized Boston, Salem, Charlestown, and certain other market towns in the province to assign certain locations in each town for the establishment of slaughterhouses and still houses for currying of leather.

Act and Resolves of the Province of Massachusetts Bay 1692-93 C. 23

"Be it ordained and enacted by the Governor, Council and Representatives convened in General Court or Assembly, and by the authority of the same,

Sect. 1 That the selectmen of the towns of Boston, Salem, and Charlestown respectively, or other market towns in the province, with two or more justices of the peace dwelling in the town, or two of the next justices of the country, shall at or before the last day of March, one thousand six hundred ninety-three, assign some certain places of the said towns (where it may be least offensive) for the erecting or setting up of slaughterhouses for the killing of all meat, still houses, and houses for trying of tallow and currying of leather (which houses may be erected of timber, the law referring to building with brick or stone not withstanding) and shall cause an entry to be made in the town book of what places shall be by them so assigned, and make known the same by posting it up in some public places of the town; by which houses and places respectively, and no other, all butchers, slaughter men, distillers, chandlers, and curriers shall exercise and practice their respective trades and mysteries; on pain that any butcher or slaughter man transgressing of this act by killing of meat in any other place, for every conviction thereof before one or more justices of the peace, shall forfeit and pay the sum of twenty shillings (shilling worth about l2-l6¢); and any distiller, chandler or currier offending against this act, for every conviction thereof before their majesties justices at the general sessions of the peace for the county, shall forfeit and pay the sum of five pounds (a pound equals 20 shillings and was worth somewhere between $2.40 and $3.20); one-third part of said forfeitures to be the use of the majesties for the support of the government of the province and incident charges thereof, one-third to the poor of the town when such offense shall be committed, and the other third to him or them that shall inform and sue for the same ....

II. Definitions

A. Accessory Structure - A detached building or structure in a secondary or subordinate capacity from the main or principal building or structure on the same premises. Example: garage behind a single-family dwelling.

B. Accessory Use - A use incidental and subordinate to the principal use of a structure. Example: a home-located physician's office.

C. Alteration - A change or rearrangement of the structural parts of a building, or an expansion or enlargement of the building.

D. Building Area - That portion of the lot remaining available for construction after all required open space and yard requirements are met.

E. Dwelling - Any enclosed space that is wholly or partially used or intended to be used for living or sleeping by human occupants provided that temporary housing shall not be regarded as a dwelling. Temporary housing is defined as any tent, trailer, mobile home, or any other shelter designed to be transportable and not attached to the ground, to another structure, or to any utility system on the same premises for more than 30 consecutive days.

F. Dwelling, Two Family - A structure containing two dwelling units and designed for occupancy by no more than two families.

G. Dwelling, Multifamily - A residential structure equipped with more than two dwelling units.

H. Dwelling Unit - Any room or group of rooms located within a dwelling and forming a single habitable unit with facilities that are used or intended to be used by a single family for living, sleeping, cooking, and eating.

I. Exception - Sometimes called "special use." An exception is a land use that can be made compatible with a district upon the imposition by the board of adjustment of special provisions covering its development, even though it would not otherwise be permitted in the district. Example: Fire substation being permitted to locate in a residential area.

J. Family - One or more individuals living together and sharing common living, sleeping, cooking, and eating facilities.

K. Home Occupation - An occupation conducted in a dwelling unit subject to the restrictions of the zoning ordinance. Limitations of interest to housing inspectors are the following: (a) Only the occupant or members of his family residing on the premises shall be engaged in the occupation, (b) the home occupation use shall be subordinate to its use for residential purposes and shall not occupy more than 25 per cent of the floor area of the dwelling unit, (c) the home occupation shall not be conducted in an accessory structure, (d) no offensive noise, glare, vibration, heat, smoke, dust, or odor shall be produced.

L. Lot- Parcel of land considered as a unit devoted to either a particular use or to occupancy by a building and its accessory structures.

M. Lot Depth - The average horizontal distance between the front and rear lot line measured at right angles to the structure.

N. Lot Width - The average horizontal distance between the sides of a lot measured at right angles to the lot depth.

O. Nonconforming Use - (a) Use of a building or use of land that does not conform to the regulations of the district in which located. (b) Nonconforming use also means a building or land use that does not conform to the regulations of the district in which the building or land is but that is nevertheless legal since it existed before enactment of the ordinance.

P. Open Space - Unoccupied space that is open to the sky and on the same lot with the building.

Q. Variance - Easing or lessening of the terms of the zoning ordinance by a public body so that relief for hardships will be provided but with the public interest still protected.

Inspectors should refer to the definitions in the zoning ordinance of their municipality for additions and changes.

III. Zoning Objectives

As stated earlier, the purpose of a zoning ordinance is to ensure that the land uses within the community are regulated not only for the health, safety, and welfare of the community but also in keeping with the comprehensive plan for community development. The objectives contained in the zoning ordinance that help to achieve a development providing for the health, safety, and welfare are the following:

A. Regulate Height, Bulk, and Area of Structure. In order to provide established standards of healthful housing within the community, regulations dealing with building heights, lot coverage, and floor areas must be established. These regulations then ensure that adequate natural lighting, ventilation, privacy, and recreational area for children will be realized. These are all fundamental physiological needs that have been determined to be necessary for a healthful environment.

    Safety from fires is enhanced because of building separations needed to meet yard and open-space requirements.

    Through prescribing minimum lot area per dwelling unit, population density controls are established.

B. Avoid Undue Levels of Noise, Vibration, Glare, Air Pollution, and Odor. By providing land use category districts, these environmental stresses upon the individual can be reduced. As in the first item, the absence of these stresses has been determined to be a fundamental physiological individual need.

C. Lessen Street Congestion Through Off-Street Parking and Off-Street Loading Requirement.

D. Facilitate Adequate Provisions of Water, Sewerage, Schools, Parks, and Playgrounds.

E. Secure Safety From Flooding.

F. Conserve Property Values. Through careful enforcement of the provisions property values will be stabilized and conserved.

IV. What Zoning Cannot Do

In order to understand more fully the difference between zoning and the other devices such as subdivision regulations, building codes, and housing ordinances, the housing inspector must know the things that cannot be accomplished by a zoning ordinance.

Items that cannot be accomplished in a zoning ordinance include:

A. Correcting Existence of Overcrowding or Substandard Housing. Zoning is not retroactive and cannot correct conditions such as those cited. These are corrected through enforcement of a minimum standards housing code.

B. Materials and Methods of Construction. Materials and methods of construction are enforced through the building codes rather than through zoning.

C. Cost of Construction. Quality of construction and hence construction costs are often regulated through deed restrictions or covenants. Zoning does, however, stabilize property values in an area by prohibiting incompatible development such as the location of a heavy industry in the midst of a well-established subdivision.

D. Subdivision Design and Layout. Design and layout of subdivisions as well as provisions for parks and streets are controlled through subdivision regulations.

V. Content of the Ordinance

Zoning ordinances establish districts of whatever size, shape, and number the municipality deems best for carrying out the purposes of the zoning ordinance. Most cities use three major districts: residential, commercial, and industrial. These three may then be subdivided into many sub districts, depending on local conditions. These districts specify the principal and accessory uses, exceptions, and prohibitions.

In general these permitted land uses are based on intensity of land use, a less intense land use being permitted in a more intense district but not vice versa. For example, a single-family residence is a less intense land use than a multifamily dwelling. A multifamily dwelling would not, however, be permitted in a single-family district.

In recent years, some ordinances are being partially based on performance standards rather than solely on land use intensity. For example, some types of industrial developments may be permitted in a less intense use district provided that the proposed land use creates no noise, glare, smoke, dust, vibration, or other environmental stress exceeding acceptable standards and provided further that adequate off street parking, screening, landscaping, and other similar measures are taken.

VI. Bulk and Height Requirements

To further achieve the earlier stated objectives of the zoning ordinance, other regulations within a particular zoning district are imposed to gain control of population densities and to provide adequate light, air, privacy, and other elements needed for a safe and healthy environment.

Most early zoning ordinances stated that within a particular district the height and bulk of any structure could not exceed certain dimensions and specified that dimensions for front, side, and rear yards must be provided. Today some zoning ordinances use floor area ratios for regulation. Floor area ratio is the relationship between the floor space of the structure and the size of the lot on which it is located. For example, a floor area ratio of 1 would permit either a two-story building covering 50 per cent of the lot, or a one-story building covering 100 per cent of the lot. This is illustrated in Figure 1. Other zoning ordinances specify the maximum amount of the lot that can be covered or else merely require that a certain amount of open space must be provided for each structure and leave the flexibility of the location to the builder. Still other ordinances, rather than specify a particular height for the structure, specify an angle of light obstruction within a particular district that will assure air and light to the surrounding structures. An example of this is shown in Figure 2.

VII. Yard Requirements

Zoning ordinances also contain yard requirements that are divided into front, rear, and side yard requirements. These requirements, in addition to stating the lot dimensions, usually designate the amount of setback

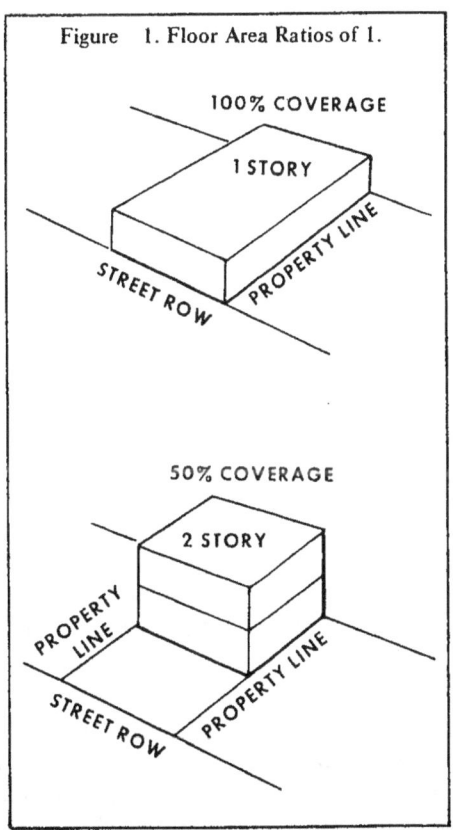

Figure 1. Floor Area Ratios of 1.

required. Most ordinances permit the erection of auxiliary buildings in rear yards provided they are located at stated distances from all lot lines and provided sufficient stated open space is maintained. If the property is a corner lot, additional requirements are set to allow visibility for motorists.

VIII. Off street Parking

Space for off street parking and off street loading is also contained in the ordinance. These requirements are based on standards relating floor space or seating capacity to land use. For example, a furniture store would require fewer off street parking spaces in relation to the floor area than a movie theater would.

IX. Nonconforming Uses

Since zoning is not retroactive, all zoning ordinances must contain a provision for nonconforming uses. If a use has already been established within a particular district before adoption of the ordinance, it must be permitted to continue. Provisions are, however, put into

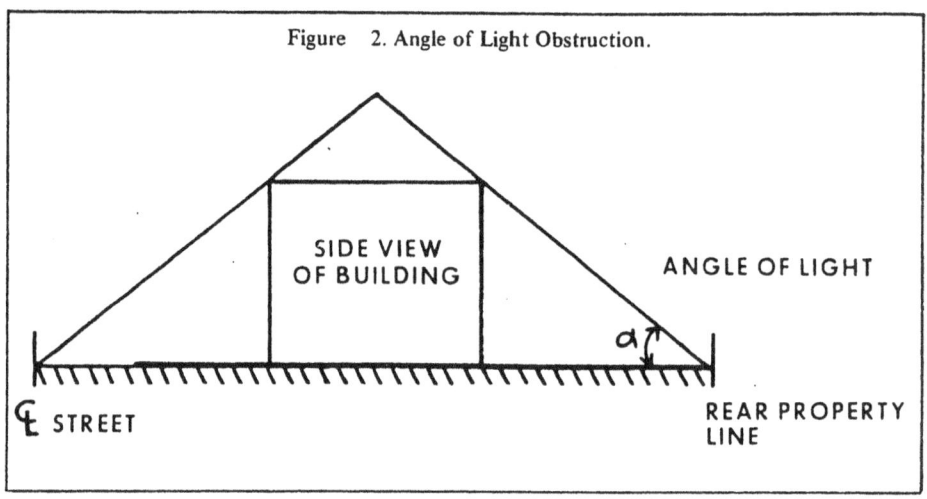

Figure 2. Angle of Light Obstruction.

The ordinance to aid in eliminating nonconforming use. These provisions generally prohibit the following: (1) An enlargement or expansion of the nonconforming uses, (2) reconstruction of the nonconforming use if more than a certain portion is destroyed, (3) resumption of the use after it has been abandoned for a period of specified time, and (4) changing the use to a higher classification or to another nonconforming use. Some zoning ordinances further provide a period of amortization during which the nonconforming land use must be phased out.

X. Variances

Zoning ordinances contain provisions for permitting variances and providing a method of granting these variances subject to certain specified conditions. A variance may be granted when, owing to a particular lot shape, topography, or other lot characteristics, an undue hardship would be imposed on the owner if the exact content of the ordinance is adhered to. For example, assume we have a piece of irregularly shaped property located in a district having the side yard requirements of 20 feet on a side and total lot size requirement of 10,000 square feet. Suppose that our property contains 10,200 feet and thus meets the area requirements; however, let us further assume that, owing to the irregular shape of the property, we can provide side yards of only 15 feet on a side. Since a hardship would be imposed if the exact letter of the law is held to, the zoning board of adjustment could be asked for a variance. Since there is sufficient total open area and since a lessening of the ordinance is not detrimental to the surrounding property, a variance would probably be granted.

Before a variance can be granted, it must be shown that (1) there is a practical hardship, (2) that the variance is needed for the owner to realize a reasonable return on the property, (3) that the original intent of the ordinance will be adhered to, (4) that the character of the neighborhood will not be changed, and (5) that the public's safety and welfare will be preserved.

XI. Exceptions

An exception is often confused with a variance. In every city there are some necessary uses that do not correspond to the permitted land uses within the district. The zoning code recognizes, however, that if proper safeguards were to be provided, these uses would not have a detrimental effect on the district. An example would be a fire substation, which could be permitted in a residential area provided the station house is designed to resemble a residential dwelling and further provided the property is properly landscaped.

XII. Administration

The key man in the zoning process is the zoning inspector, since he must come in contact with each case. In many cases the zoning inspector may also be the building inspector or the housing inspector. Since the building inspector or housing inspector is already in the field making inspections, it is relatively easy for him to check compliance with a zoning ordinance. This compliance can be checked by comparing the actual land use against that allowed for the area and shown on the zoning map.

Each zoning ordinance has a map as a part of the ordinance giving the permitted usage for each block. By taking a copy of this map with him, the inspector can make a preliminary check of the land use in the field. If the use does not conform, the inspector must then check with the Zoning Board to see if the property in question was a "nonconforming use" at the time of passage of the ordinance and if an exception has been granted. In cities where up-to-date records of existing nonconforming uses and exceptions granted are maintained, the inspector can check the use in the field against the records.

When violation is observed and the property owner is duly notified of the violation, he then has the right of hearing before a Zoning Board of Adjustment (sometimes also called the Zoning Board of Appeals). The Board may uphold the zoning enforcement officer or may rule in favor of the property owner. If the action of the zoning enforcement officer is upheld, the property owner may, if he so desires, seek relief through the courts; otherwise the violation will be corrected to conform to the zoning code.

XIII. How Zoning Can Benefit the Housing Inspector

It is of critical importance for the housing inspector, the building inspector, and the zoning inspector to work closely together in cities where these positions and responsibilities are separate. Experience has shown that when illegal conversions or uses of properties occur, these illegally converted properties are often among the most substandard encountered in the city and often contain especially dangerous housing code violations.

In communities where the zoning code is enforced effectively, the resulting zoning compliance in new and existing housing helps advance, as well as sustain, many of the minimum standards of the housing code such as occupancy, ventilation, light, and unimpeded egress. By the same token, building or housing inspectors can often aid the zoning inspector by helping eliminate some nonconforming uses through code enforcement.

XIV. Example of Zoning and Housing Relationships

The following cases will illustrate these relationships:

A Case 1

Two and one-half-story, 13-room house. Originally it had these features:

a Five-room dwelling unit on first floor including a three-piece bathroom.

b Eight-room dwelling unit occupying the second and third floors including one bathroom of three pieces on the second floor. The second and third floors are served by only one staircase.

c Two oil burners, one heating first floor, the other the second and third floors.

It is located in a residential zoning district where two-family housing is the maximum use permitted.

Five years later, while making a regular inspection, the zoning officer found this house in the process of being converted into a three-family use in violation of the zoning ordinance. The owner has already done these things.

a   Made second floor into a separate five-room dwelling unit.

b   Started converting the three rooms on the third floor into another apartment by:

  1. Installing a three-piece bathroom, 35 square feet in area, against the windowless west wall of the center bedroom, the habitable area being thus reduced to 40 square feet, and setting up the remainder of the area as the living room by providing a coffee table, lamp, and two overstuffed chairs;

  2. Putting in a wall kitchenette consisting of a sink with cold water and a stove, plus a table, lamp, and cupboards in the rear bedroom that is 60 square feet in area;

  3. Equipping the front bedroom that is 90 square feet in size with two beds, chest of drawers, and other bedroom furnishings for two.

He admitted, however, that he had not checked on state tenement house law requirements since he did not realize multiple dwellings of three families or more are covered by this law.

Question: How many violations (either housing or zoning) can you find?

Answer: As a result of these actions by the owner, the house now has one more dwelling unit than is permitted by the zoning ordinance in this residential district and also contains these obvious housing code violations:

(a) Threatened over occupancy of the third-floor dwelling unit (only 190 square feet available, but 250 square feet habitable floor space is the minimum required for two occupants).

(b) Size of the front bedroom inadequate by 30 square feet if it is used by two occupants. The back bedroom lacks the requirements needed for occupancy by one person (70 square feet). If a third person lived in the dwelling unit the minimum required habitable floor area would then become 350 square feet.

(c) The bathroom does not meet the light and ventilation requirements.

(d) The kitchen sink does not have hot water.

(e) No refrigerator is provided.

(f) From the description it sounds as if one might have to go through a sleeping room to reach the bathroom. This would be a violation.

(g) Both the second and third floor units are in violation since they lack two means of egress.

B Case 2

Assume that a three-family dwelling unit is the largest size permitted in the zoning district where the building in question is located. The housing inspector's investigation of the three-story dwelling from cellar to roof showed that it contained:

1. Four dwelling units, two with six rooms each and two with three rooms each.

2. Five families, three in separate dwelling units and the two on the third floor in one unit.

3. A bathroom and a kitchen on the second floor shared by two families.

4. The bathroom and kitchen on the third floor also being shared by two families.

5. Inadequate means of egress from the dwelling unit in the third floor.

Question: If you were the housing inspector, what actions would you take?

Answer: In this situation there are definite housing code violations. The housing inspector also knows there is a zoning violation. Because he knows that the property must meet zoning requirements before complying with the housing code, the inspector would refer this case to the zoning department for action.

The housing inspector should never speak for the zoning department and tell the owner that he is in violation of a zoning ordinance unless he and the zoning inspector are the same individual. The housing inspector should complete his housing inspection and leave. Responsibility for informing the owner of any zoning violation lies with the zoning department.

In this particular case, some housing code violations will be corrected through enforcement of zoning. However, there are still violations of requirements for egress, a third kitchen, and a third bathroom.

After compliance with the zoning ordinance has been obtained, the zoning department should notify the housing inspector so that he can then enforce any housing violations that may still exist.

C Case 3

Mr. Jones, a zoning inspector, gets a report that at 1212 Oak Street the owner, Mr. Smith, is converting his single-family house into two apartments and has already started alterations. Investigations of the zoning map shows that in this district, apartments, up to four, are permitted if 1,500 square feet of open land area is provided for each apartment. Mr. Jones checks and finds that no building permit has been issued. A site investigation reveals that Mr. Smith has only 2,000 square feet of open area available. He then informs Mr. Smith that he is in violation of the zoning ordinance.

Mr. Smith then appeals to the Zoning Board of Adjustment for a variance to allow him to have two apartments even though he does not have the required 3,000 square feet 0 f open area. His appeal is denied by the board since no real hardship exists. As a result, Mr. Smith must rent the property as a single-family dwelling and is unable to recover the money he has already spent in starting alterations.

Discuss:

1. The actions of Mr. Jones.

Answer: Mr. Jones was justified in citing Mr. Smith for a zoning violation since the proposed open area would have been inadequate.

2 The action of the Board of Adjustment.

Answer: The Board of Adjustment was also justified in upholding the zoning regulations. If the board had not acted in this manner, the crowding on this property could well have started deterioration in surrounding properties.

3 The action of Mr. Smith.

Answer: Mr. Smith had no legitimate complaint when the Board ruled against him. If he had first sought to obtain a building permit, as required by law, he would have been told that his proposed alterations would not meet zoning regulations and hence would not have suffered a monetary loss.

D Case 4

Mr. Edwards requests a building permit to change a three-story single-family house into a two-family unit. Since two-family units are permitted in this district and he has sufficient open area, the permit is granted.

Six months later, the housing inspector, while making a systematic code enforcement inspection, finds that the converted house now has an apartment on each of the three floors. The bath on the second floor is shared by families on the second and third floors. This is a violation of the housing code.

Knowing that all the other houses on this street are only one- or two-family units, he also suspects a zoning violation. After returning to the office, he contacts the zoning department and learns that Mr. Edwards is in violation of the zoning ordinance as well as of the housing code.

Question: Which ordinance must be enforced first and why?

Answer: The zoning ordinance must be enforced first, since a zoning ordinance is a "primary" ordinance and determines the land use of a particular property. A housing code ordinance is a "secondary" ordinance and sets standards of residential usage on the property.

E Case 5

During a routine inspection, the housing inspector finds a house with three families, one of which is living in a cellar apartment.

Question: What actions should he take?

Answer: The inspector should immediately cite the owner for a violation of the ordinance and then follow through to see that the situation is corrected. If the family living in the cellar requires housing assistance as a result of corrective measures taken, the housing inspector should inform them of public agencies available for assistance.

F Case 6

During a routine inspection of a district zoned for up to three-family use, the housing inspector encounters a house that the owner says contains two dwelling units in addition to his own, and also one rooming unit. The inspector finds a cook stove in the "rooming unit."

Question: What actions should he take?

Answer: Although a rooming unit would be permitted in this district, the addition of a cook stove changes the rooming unit into a dwelling unit.

The inspector should refer this case to the zoning department for immediate action and then follow up for housing violations at a later date.

G Case 7

The housing inspector is investigating a complaint of alleged housing violations. The owner refuses to admit the inspector inside the building and becomes belligerent.

Question: What should the inspector do next?

Answer: The inspector should remain courteous and not lose his temper. If the inspector is not able to obtain permission to inspect without further arousing the owner, he should leave.

Since recent decisions of the U.S. Supreme Court have dictated the inclusion of requirements to obtain a search warrant in cases where entry to the inspector is denied, the inspector should obtain a warrant. He will then return at a later time with someone to serve the warrant.

H   Case 8

During an inspection in July, the housing inspector finds a house that has been converted into two apartments. While checking the basement, he sees that the furnace appears in an unsafe condition. Further checking reveals that there is no provision for heat in the second apartment.

Question: What action should the inspector take since it is July and heat is not now needed. Besides, how does he know that the owner will not install heat before winter?

Answer: The inspector should cite the owner for a violation of the housing code anyway. In his notice of violations, because it is July, he can give the owner sufficient time to comply. He would also send a copy of the letter to the heating inspector for follow up.

I   Case 9

During an inspection, the housing inspector is greeted at the door by a 10-year-old boy who is alone. The boy says it is all right to make the inspection.

Question: Should he? Why?

Answer: No. Permission to enter must be obtained from a responsible adult. Suppose that instead of the 10-year-old boy, he had found a 16-year-old girl.

Question: How would these change things? Why?

Answer: It would not change things, since the 16-year-old girl is not considered a responsible adult. For the protection of the inspector, some housing departments would not permit him to enter alone when the house is occupied by only a female, especially one under age.

J   Case 10

During his inspections the housing inspector finds a house that has no bathroom but does have an outside pit privy.

Question: What action should be taken?

Answer: The inspector should issue a violation for lack of indoor toilet facilities and follow through the regular steps established. by his housing department. A copy of the violation should also be sent to the health department for any actions that they may wish to take for elimination of the privy.

K   Case 11

A number of violations are found in a residence, but the family is occupying the unit under a land purchase contract agreement with the landlord. The owner holds title until enough rent is paid to equal the sale price. The repairs needed are more than the family can afford and are such that the building should be declared unfit for occupancy. The family now has $2,000 worth of equity in the property.

Questions: What actions should the inspector take? Who is responsible for repairs? Who will lose money?

Answer: The inspector would cite the owner of record for a housing violation, since the owner of record is responsible for repairs. If the owner will not bring the building into compliance with the code, the building should be posted as unfit for habitation and the family removed.

The family buying will probably lose in this situation. Before contracting to buy, they should have obtained a certificate of inspection from the housing department showing any violations existing at the time of purchase.

L Case 12

The property at 112 East Street is owned by an out-of-state individual. The housing inspector found the property unfit for habitation and has had the family renting the property removed. The house is now vacant and the out-of-town owners will not make the repairs since the cost of the necessary

repairs would be too great in relation to the value of the property. The property is in an area that will probably be included in a future urban renewal project within the next few years.

Complaints have been made to the housing department by the neighbors that the house has its windows broken out and its doors broken open. Children play inside during the day and have almost set the building on fire several times. Moreover, vagrants occasionally sleep inside at night.

Question: What action would you take if you were the housing inspector?

Answer: After following standard department procedures, the housing inspector should recommend, that the house be demolished and this cost assessed as a lien against the property. If allowed to remain, the house will be a detriment to surrounding properties and also to the neighborhood.

M Case 13

During a routine inspection, you find a house with very poor premises sanitation and evidence of roaches, flies, and rats. The property meets minimum housing standards otherwise.

Question: What action can you take?

Answer: The action depends on local regulations and procedures. In many communities the housing program is organizationally located within the health department. In that case, the housing inspector would probably follow through in requiring elimination of the infestation. If the housing inspection program were located within a department other than the health department, the housing inspector may refer the case to the health department for action.

N Case 14

While making a systematic code inspection, the housing inspector encounters a lady who questions the inspector regarding his findings on the house next door, which she is sure is much worse than hers.

Question: How should the inspector deal with the lady?

Answer: The inspector must be very courteous and tactful in his conversation and inform her that he is not permitted to discuss his survey findings for other properties.

BASIC FUNDAMENTALS OF DRAWINGS AND SPECIFICATIONS

A building project may be broadly divided into two major phases: (1) the DESIGN phase, and (2) the CONSTRUCTION phase. In accordance with a number of considerations, of which the function and desired appearance of the building are perhaps the most important, the architect first conceives the building in his mind's eye, as it were, and then sets his concept down on paper in the form of PRESENTATION drawings. Presentation drawings are usually done in PERSPECTIVE, by employing the PICTORIAL drawing techniques.

Next the architect and the engineer, working together, decide upon the materials to be used in the structure and the construction methods which are to be followed. The engineer determines the loads which supporting members will carry and the strength qualities the members must have to bear the loads. He also designs the mechanical systems of the structure, such as the lighting, heating, and plumbing systems. The end-result of all this is the preparation of architectural and engineering DESIGN SKETCHES. The purpose of these sketches is to guide draftsmen in the preparation of CONSTRUCTION DRAWINGS.

The construction drawings, plus the SPECIFICATIONS to be described later, are the chief sources of information for the supervisors and craftsman responsible for the actual work of construction. Construction drawings consist mostly of ORTHOGRAPHIC views, prepared by draftsmen who employ the standard technical drawing techniques, and who use the symbols and other designations

You should make a thorough study of symbols before proceeding further with this chapter. Figure 1 illustrates the conventional symbols for the more common types of material used on structures. Figure 2 shows the more common symbols used for doors and windows.

Before you can interpret construction drawings correctly, you must also have some knowledge of the structure and of the terminology for common structural members.

I. STRUCTURES

The main parts of a structure are the LOAD-BEARING STRUCTURAL MEMBERS, which support and transfer the loads on the structure while remaining in equilibrium with each other. The places where members are connected to other members are called JOINTS. The sum total of the load supported by the structural members at a particular instant is equal to the total DEAD LOAD plus the total LIVE LOAD.

The total dead load is the total weight of the structure, which gradually increases, of course, as the structure rises, and remains constant once it is completed. The total live load is the total weight of movable objects (such as people, furniture, bridge traffic or the like) which the structure happens to be supporting at a particular instant.

The live loads in a structure are transmitted through the various load-bearing structural members to the ultimate support of the earth as follows. Immediate or direct support for the live loads is provided by HORIZTONAL members; these are in turn supported by VERTICAL members; which in turn are supported by FOUNDATIONS and/or FOOTINGS; and these are, finally, supported by the earth.

The ability of the earth to support a load is called the SOIL BEARING CAPACITY; it is determined by test and measured in pounds per square foot. Soil bearing capacity varies considerably with different types of soil, and a soil of given bearing capacity will bear a heavier load on a wide foundation or footing than it will on a narrow one.

VERTICAL STRUCTURAL MEMBERS

Vertical structural members are high-strength columns; they are sometimes called PILLARS in buildings. Outside wall columns and inside bottom-floor columns, usually rest directly on footings. Outside-wall columns usually extend from the footing or foundation to the roof line. Inside bottom-floor columns extend upward from footings or foundations to horizontal members which in turn support the

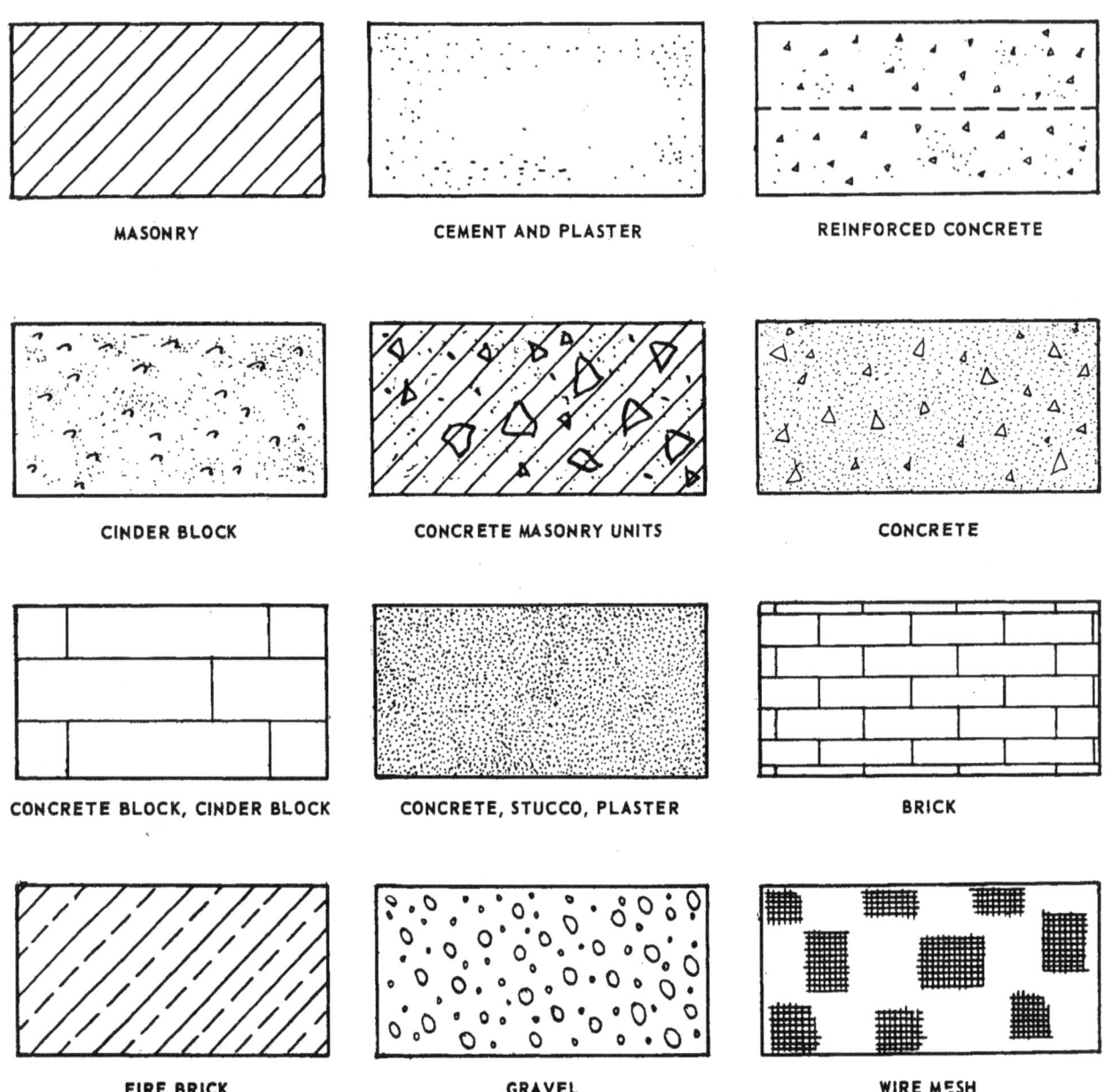

Figure 1.—Material symbols.

first floor. Upper floor columns usually are located directly over lower floor columns.

A PIER in building construction might be called a short column. It may rest directly on a footing, or it may be simply set or driven in the ground. Building piers usually support the lowermost horizontal structural members.

In bridge construction a pier is a vertical member which provides intermediate support for the bridge superstructure.

The chief vertical structural members in light frame construction are called STUDS. They are supported on horizontal members called SILLS or SOLE PLATES, and are topped by horizontal members called TOP PLATES or RAFTER PLATES. CORNER POSTS are enlarged studs, as it were, located at the building corners. In early FULL-FRAME construction a corner post was usually a solid piece of larger timber. In most modern construction BUILT-UP

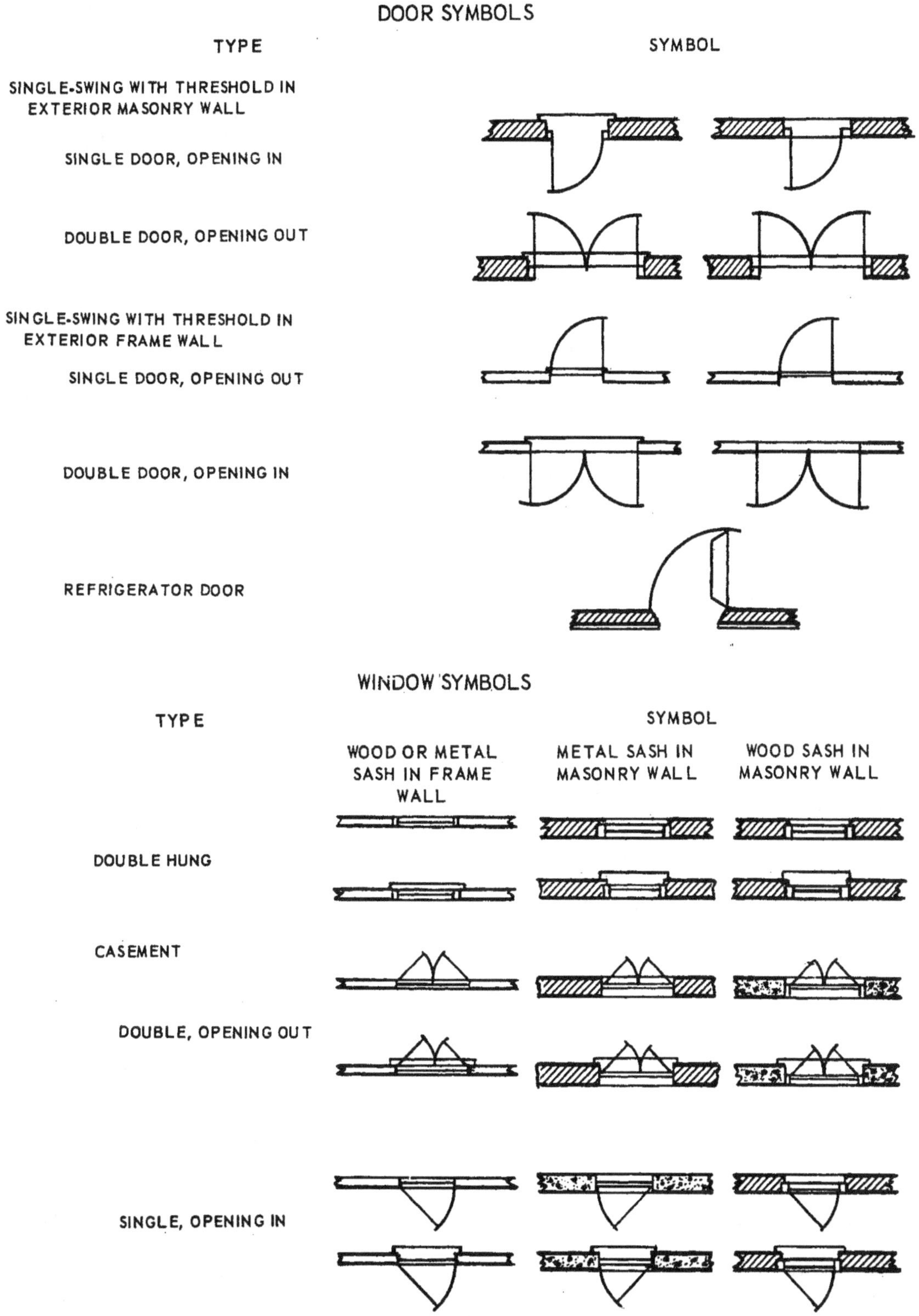

DOOR SYMBOLS

TYPE	SYMBOL
SINGLE-SWING WITH THRESHOLD IN EXTERIOR MASONRY WALL	
SINGLE DOOR, OPENING IN	
DOUBLE DOOR, OPENING OUT	
SINGLE-SWING WITH THRESHOLD IN EXTERIOR FRAME WALL	
SINGLE DOOR, OPENING OUT	
DOUBLE DOOR, OPENING IN	
REFRIGERATOR DOOR	

WINDOW SYMBOLS

TYPE	SYMBOL		
	WOOD OR METAL SASH IN FRAME WALL	METAL SASH IN MASONRY WALL	WOOD SASH IN MASONRY WALL
DOUBLE HUNG			
CASEMENT			
DOUBLE, OPENING OUT			
SINGLE, OPENING IN			

Figure 2 — Architectural symbols (door and windows).

corner posts are used, consisting of various numbers of ordinary studs, nailed together in various ways.

HORIZONTAL STRUCTURAL MEMBERS

In technical terminology, a horizontal load-bearing structural member which spans a space, and which is supported at both ends, is called a BEAM. A member which is FIXED at one end only is called a CANTILEVER. Steel members which consist of solid pieces of the regular structural steel shapes are called beams, but a type of steel member which is actually a light truss is called an OPEN-WEB STEEL JOIST or a BAR STEEL JOIST.

Horizontal structural members which support the ends of floor beams or joists in wood frame construction are called SILLS, GIRTS, or GIRDERS, depending on the type of framing being done and the location of the member in the structure. Horizontal members which support studs are called SILL or SOLE PLATES. Horizontal members which support the wall-ends of rafters are called RAFTER PLATES. Horizontal members which assume the weight of concrete or masonry walls above door and window openings are called LINTELS.

TRUSSES

A beam of given strength, without intermediate supports below, can support a given load over only a certain maximum span. If the span is wider than this maximum, intermediate supports, such as a column must be provided for the beam. Sometimes it is not feasible or possible to install intermediate supports. When such is the case, a TRUSS may be used instead of a beam.

A beam consists of a single horizontal member. A truss, however, is a framework, consisting of two horizontal (or nearly horizontal) members, joined together by a number of vertical and/or inclined members. The horizontal members are called the UPPER and LOWER CHORDS; the vertical and/or inclined members are called the WEB MEMBERS.

ROOF MEMBERS

The horizontal or inclined members which provide support to a roof are called RAFTERS. The lengthwise (right angle to the rafters) member which support the peak ends of the rafters in a roof is called the RIDGE. (The ridge may be called the Ridge board, the Ridge PIECE, or the Ridge pole.) Lengthwise members other than ridges are called PURLINS. In wood frame construction the wall ends of rafters are supported on horizontal members called RAFTER PLATES, which are in turn supported by the outside wall studs. In concrete or masonry wall construction, the wall ends of rafters may be anchored directly on the walls, or on plates bolted to the walls.

II. CONSTRUCTION DRAWINGS

Construction drawings are drawings in which as much construction information as possible is presented GRAPHICALLY, or by means of pictures. Most construction drawings consist of ORTHOGRAPHIC views. GENERAL drawings consist of PLANS AND ELEVATIONS, drawn on a relatively small scale. DETAIL drawings consist of SECTIONS and DETAILS, drawn on a relatively large scale.

PLANS

A PLAN view is, as you know, a view of an object or area as it would appear if projected onto a horizontal plane passed through or held above the object or area. The most common construction plans are PLOT PLANS (also called SITE PLANS), FOUNDATION PLANS, FLOOR PLANS, and FRAMING PLANS.

A PLOT PLAN shows the contours, boundaries, roads, utilities, trees, structures, and any other significant physical features pertaining to or located on the site. The locations of proposed structures are indicated by appropriate outlines or floor plans. By locating the corners of a proposed structure at given distances from a REFERENCE or BASE line (which is shown on the plan and which can be located on the site), the plot plan provides essential data for those who will lay out the building lines. By indicating the elevations of existing and proposed earth surfaces (by means of CONTOUR lines), the plot plan provides essential data for the graders and excavators.

A FOUNDATION PLAN (fig. 3) is a plan view of a structure projected on a horizontal plane passed through (in imagination, of course) at the level of the tops of the foundations. The plan shown in figure 3 tells you that the main foundation of this structure will consist of a rectangular 12-in. concrete block wall, 22 ft

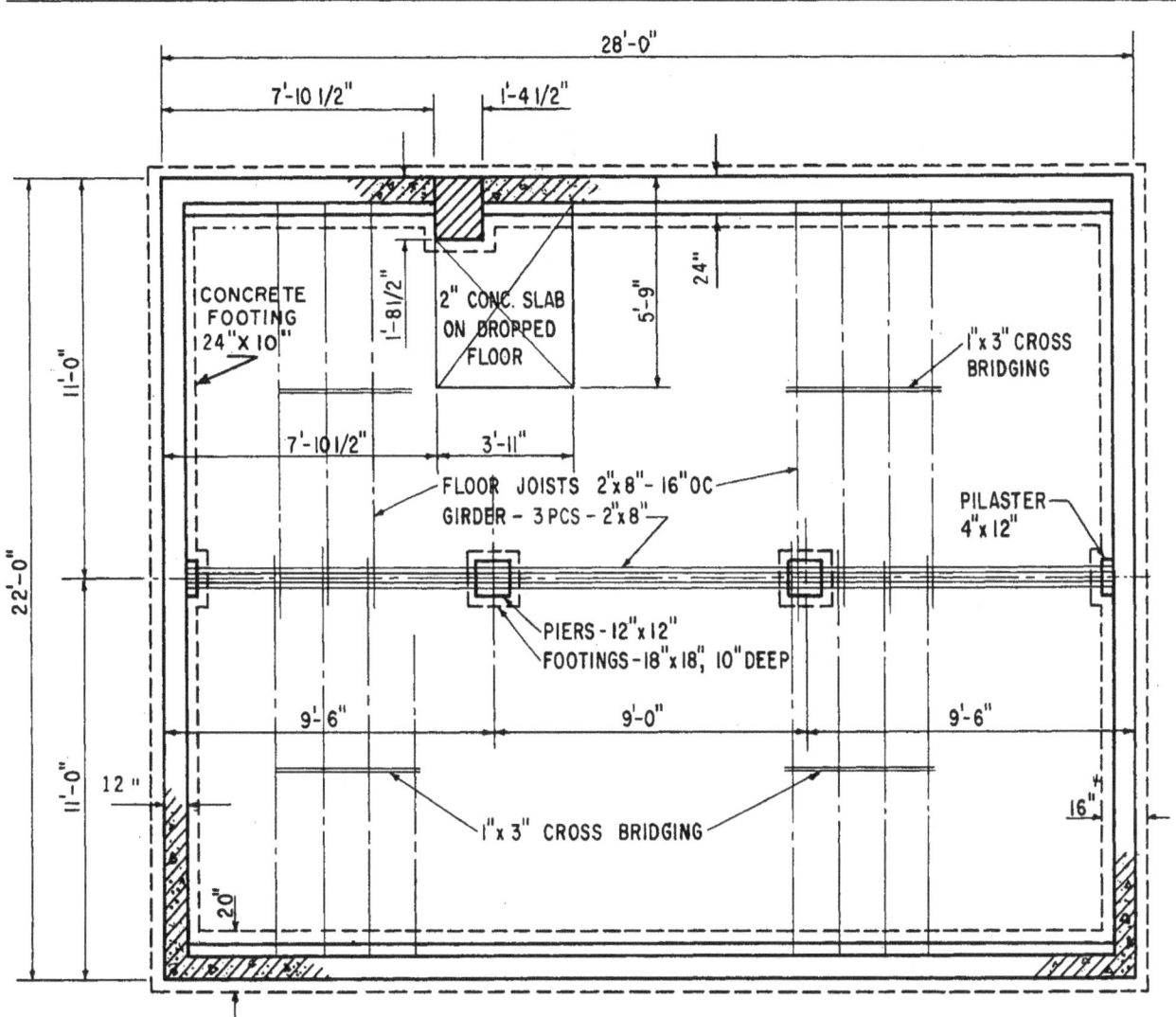

Figure 3.—Foundation plan.

wide by 28 ft long, centered on a concrete footing 24 in. wide. Besides the outside wall and footing, there will be two 12-in. square piers, centered on 18-in. square footings, and located on center 9 ft 6 in. from the end wall building lines. These piers will support a ground floor center-line girder.

A FLOOR PLAN (also called a BUILDING PLAN) is developed as shown in figure 4. Information on a floor plan includes the lengths, thicknesses, and character of the building walls at that particular floor, the widths and locations of door and window openings, the lengths and character of partitions, the number and arrangement of rooms, and the types and locations of utility installations. A typical floor plan is shown in figure 5.

FRAMING PLANS show the dimensions, numbers, and arrangement of structural members in wood frame construction. A simple FLOOR FRAMING PLAN is superimposed on the foundation plan shown in figure 3. From this foundation plan you learn that the ground-floor joists in this structure will consist of 2 x 8's, lapped at the girder, and spaced 16 in. O. C. The plan also shows that each row of joists is to be braced by a row of 1 x 3 cross bridging. For a more complicated floor framing problem, a framing plan like the one shown in figure 2-6 would be required. This plan

  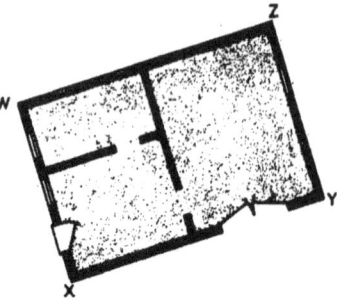

PERSPECTIVE VIEW OF A BUILDING SHOWING CUTTING PLANE WXY

PREVIOUS PERSPECTIVE VIEW AT CUTTING PLANE WXYZ, TOP REMOVED

DEVELOPED FLOOR PLAN WXYZ

Figure 4.—Floor plan development.

shows, among other things, the arrangement of joists and other members around stair wells and other floor openings.

A WALL FRAMING PLAN gives similar information with regard to the studs, corner posts, bracing, sills, plates, and other structural members in the walls. Since it is a view on a vertical plane, a wall framing plan is not a plan in the strict technical sense. However, the practice of calling it a plan has become a general custom. A ROOF FRAMING PLAN gives similar information with regard to the rafters, ridge, purlins, and other structural members in the roof.

A UTILITY PLAN is a floor plan which shows the layout of a heating, electrical, plumbing, or other utility system. Utility plans are used primarily by the ratings responsible for the utilities, but they are important to the Builder as well. Most utility installations require the leaving of openings in walls, floors, and roofs for the admission or installation of utility features. The Builder who is placing a concrete foundation wall must study the utility plans to determine the number, sizes, and locations of the openings he must leave for utilities.

Figure 7 shows a heating plan. Figure 8 shows an electrical plan.

ELEVATIONS

ELEVATIONS show the front, rear, and sides of a structure projected on vertical planes parallel to the planes of the sides. Front, rear, right side, and left side elevations of a small building are shown in figure 9.

As you can see, the elevations give you a number of important vertical dimensions, such as the perpendicular distance from the finish floor to the top of the rafter plate and from the finish floor to the tops of door and window finished openings. They also show the locations and characters of doors and windows. Dimensions of window sash and dimensions and character of lintels, however, are usually set forth in a WINDOW SCHEDULE.

A SECTION view is a view of a cross-section, developed as indicated in figure 10. By general custom, the term is confined to views of cross-sections cut by vertical planes. A floor plan or foundation plan, cut by a horizontal plane, is, technically speaking, a section view as well as a plan view, but it is seldom called a section.

The most important sections are the WALL sections. Figure 11 shows three wall sections for three alternate types of construction for the building shown in figures 3, 5, 7 and 8. The angled arrows marked "A" in figure 5 indicate the location of the cutting plane for the sections.

The wall sections are of primary importance to the supervisors of construction and to the craftsmen who will do the actual building. Take the first wall section, marked "masonry construction," for example. Starting at the bottom, you learn that the footing will be concrete, 2 ft wide and 10 in. high. The vertical distance of the bottom of the footing below FINISHED GRADE (level of the finished earth surface around the house) "varies"—meaning that it will depend on the soil-bearing capacity at the particular site. The foundation wall will consist of

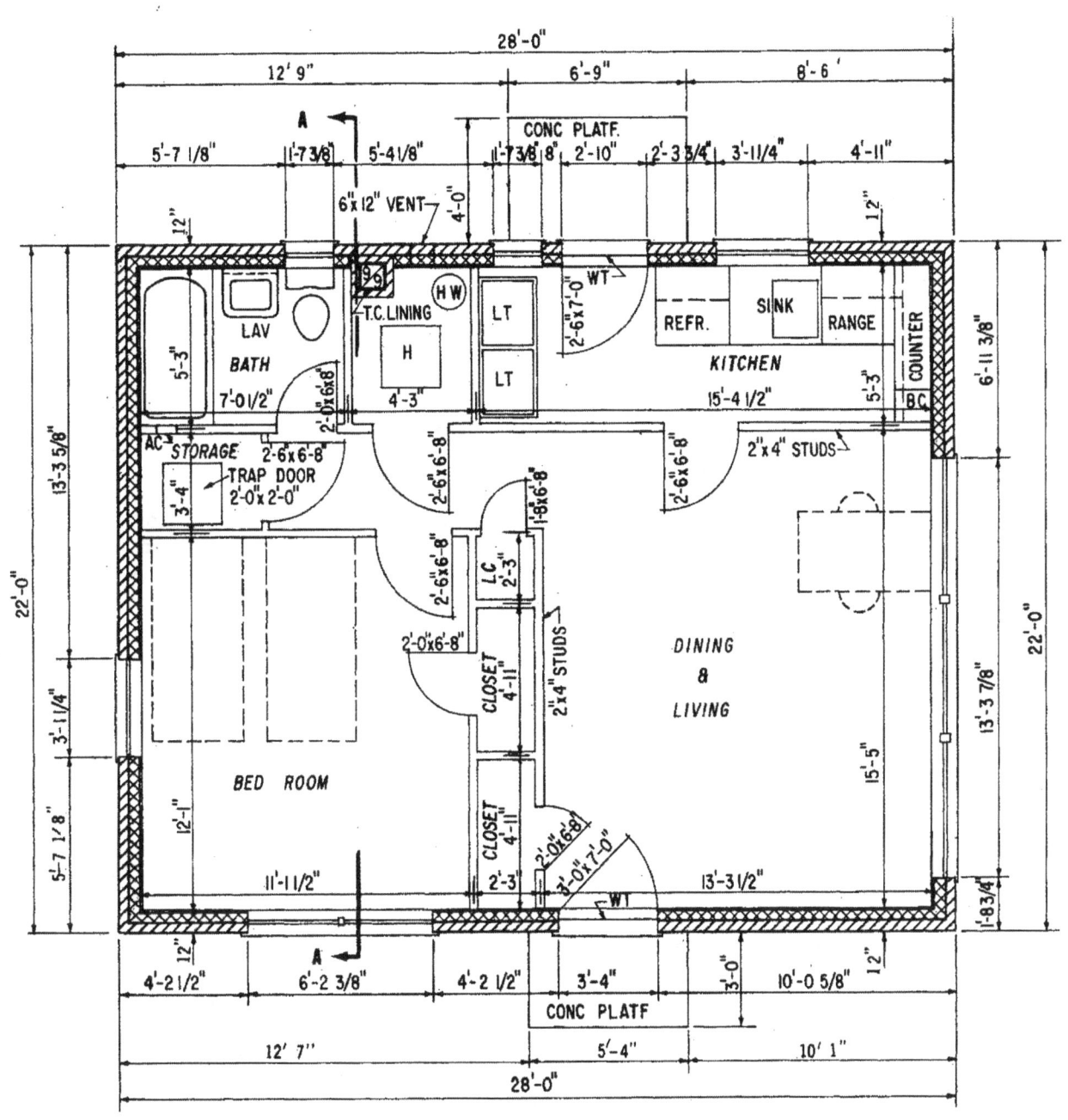

Figure 5.—Floor plan.

12-in. CMU, centered on the footing. Twelve-inch blocks will extend up to an unspecified distance below grade, where a 4-in. brick FACING (dimension indicated in the middle wall section) begins. Above the line of the bottom of the facing, it is obvious that 8-in. instead of 12-in. blocks will be used in the foundation wall.

The building wall above grade will consist of a 4-in. brick FACING TIER, backed by a BACKING TIER of 4-in. cinder blocks. The floor joists, consisting of 2 x 8's placed 16 in. O.C., will be anchored on 2 x 4 sills bolted to the top of the foundation wall. Every third joist will be additionally secured by a 2 x 1/4 STRAP ANCHOR embedded in the cinder block backing tier of the building wall.

The window (window B in the plan front elevation, fig. 9) will have a finished opening

DRAWINGS AND SPECIFICATIONS

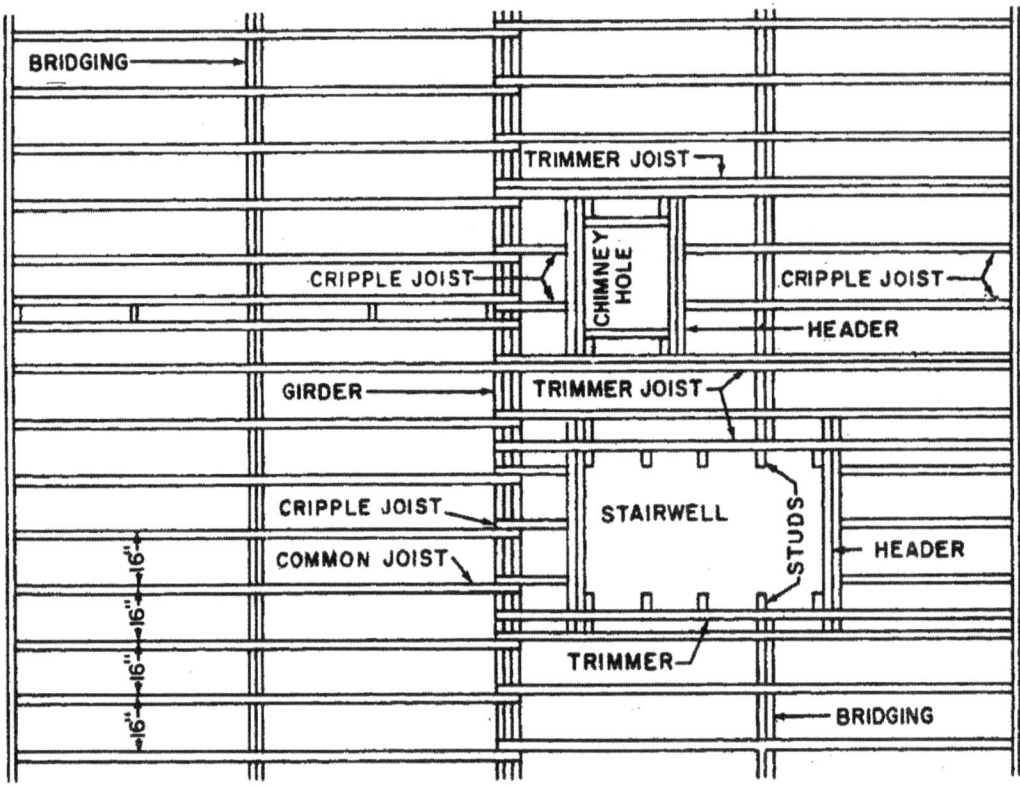

Figure 6.—Floor framing plan.

4 ft 2-5/8 in. high. The bottom of the opening will come 2 ft 11-3/4 in. above the line of the finished floor. As indicated in the wall section, (fig. 11) 13 masonry COURSES (layers of masonry units) above the finished floor line will amount to a vertical distance of 2 ft 11-3/4 in. As also indicated, another 19 courses will amount to the prescribed vertical dimension of the finished window opening.

Window framing details, including the placement and cross-sectional character of the lintel, are shown. The building wall will be carried 10-1/4 in., less the thickness of a 2 x 8 RAFTER PLATE, above the top of the window finished opening. The total vertical distance from the top of the finished floor to the top of the rafter plate will be 8 ft 2-1/4 in. Ceiling joists and rafters will consist of 2 x 6's, and the roof covering will consist of composition shingles laid on wood sheathing.

Flooring will consist of a wood finisher floor laid on a wood subfloor. Inside walls will be finished with plaster on lath (except on masonry wall which would be with or without lath as directed). A minimum of 2 vertical feet of crawl space will extend below the bottoms of the floor joists.

The middle wall section in figure 2-11 gives you similar information for a similar building constructed with wood frame walls and a DOUBLE-HUNG window. The third wall section shown in the figure gives you similar information for a similar building constructed with a steel frame, a casement window, and a concrete floor finished with asphalt tile.

DETAILS

DETAIL drawings are drawings which are done on a larger scale than that of the general drawings, and which show features not appearing at all, or appearing on too small a scale, on the general drawings. The wall sections just described are details as well as sections, since

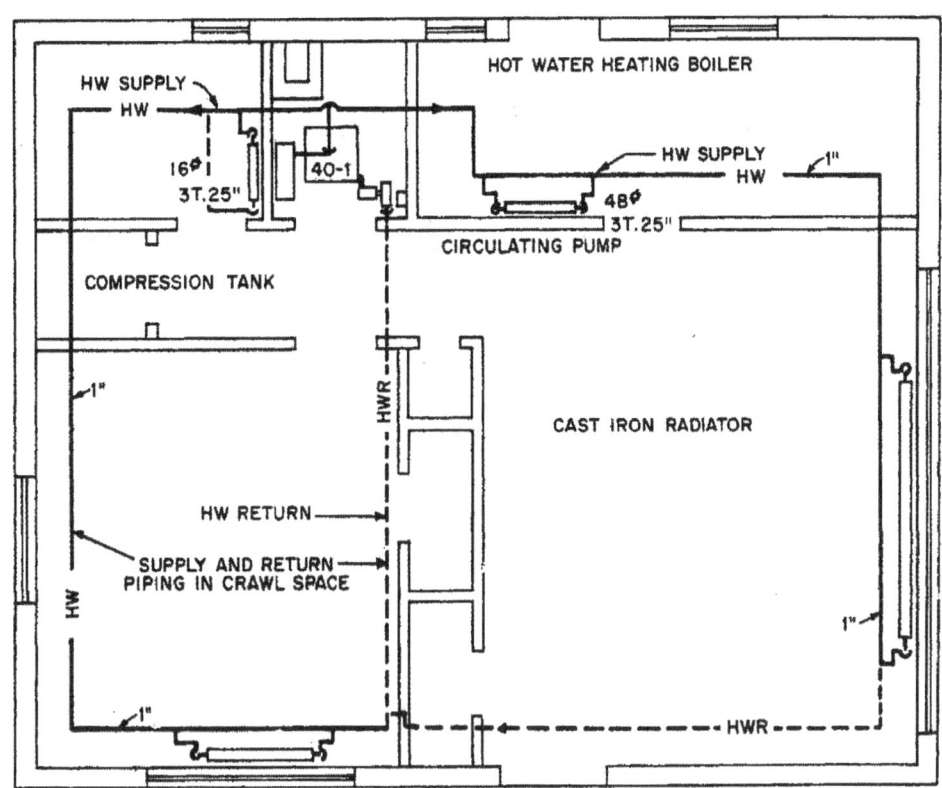

Figure 7.—Heating plan.

they are drawn on a considerable larger scale than the plans and elevations. Framing details at doors, windows, and cornices, which are the most common types of details, are practically always sections.

Details are included whenever the information given in the plans, elevations, and wall sections is not sufficiently "detailed" to guide the craftsmen on the job. Figure 12 shows some typical door and window wood framing details, and an eave detail for a very simple type of CORNICE. You should study these details closely to learn the terminology of framing members.

III. SPECIFICATIONS

The construction drawings contain much of the information about a structure which can be presented GRAPHICALLY (that is, in drawings). A very considerable amount of information can be presented this way, but there is more information which the construction supervisors and artisans must have and which is not adaptable to the graphic form of presentation. Information of this kind includes quality criteria for materials (maximum amounts of aggregate per sack of cement, for example), specified standards of workmanship, prescribed construction methods, and the like.

Information of this kind is presented in a list of written SPECIFICATIONS, familiarly known as the "SPECS." A list of specifications usually begins with a section on GENERAL CONDITIONS. This section starts with a GENERAL DESCRIPTION of the building, including the type of foundation, type or types of windows, character of framing, utilities to be installed, and the like. Next comes a list of DEFINITIONS of terms used in the specs, and next certain routine declarations of responsibility and certain conditions to be maintained on the job.

SPECIFIC CONDITIONS are grouped in sections under headings which describe each of the major construction phases of the job. Separate specifications are written for each phase, and the phases are then combined to more or less follow the usual order of construction sequences on the job. A typical list of sections under "Specific Conditions" follows:

DRAWINGS AND SPECIFICATIONS

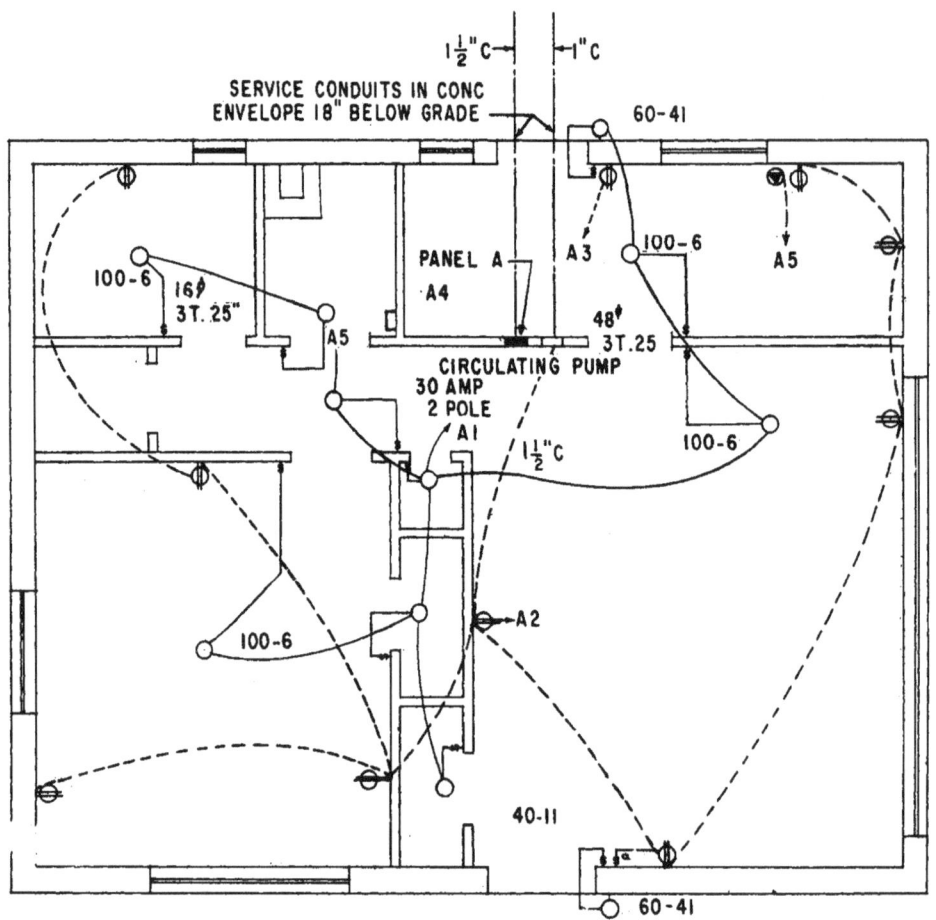

Figure 8.—Electrical plan.

2.—EARTHWORK 3.—CONCRETE 4.—MASONRY 5.—MISCELLANEOUS STEEL AND IRON 6.—CARPENTRY AND JOINERY 7.—LATHING AND PLASTERING 8.—TILE WORK 9.—FINISH FLOORING 10.—GLAZING 11.—FINISHING HARDWARE 12.—PLUMBING 13.—HEATING 14.—ELECTRICAL WORK 15.—FIELD PAINTING.

A section under "Specific Conditions" usually begins with a subsection of GENERAL REQUIREMENTS which apply to the phase of construction being considered. Under Section 6, CARPENTRY AND JOINERY, for example, the first section might go as follows:

6-01. GENERAL REQUIREMENTS. All framing, rough carpentry, and finishing woodwork required for the proper completion of the building shall be provided. All woodwork shall be protected from the weather, and the building shall be thoroughly dry before the finish is placed. All finish shall be dressed, smoothed, and sandpapered at the mill, and in addition shall be hand smoothed and sandpapered at the building where necessary to produce proper finish. Nailing shall be done, as far as practicable, in concealed places, and all nails in finishing work shall be set. All lumber shall be S4S (meaning, "surfaced on 4 sides"); all materials for millwork and finish shall be kiln-dried; all rough and framing lumber shall be air- or kiln-dried. Any cutting, fitting, framing, and blocking necessary for the accommodation of other work shall be provided. All nails, spikes, screws, bolts, plates, clips, and other fastenings and rough hardware necessary for the proper completion of the building shall be provided.

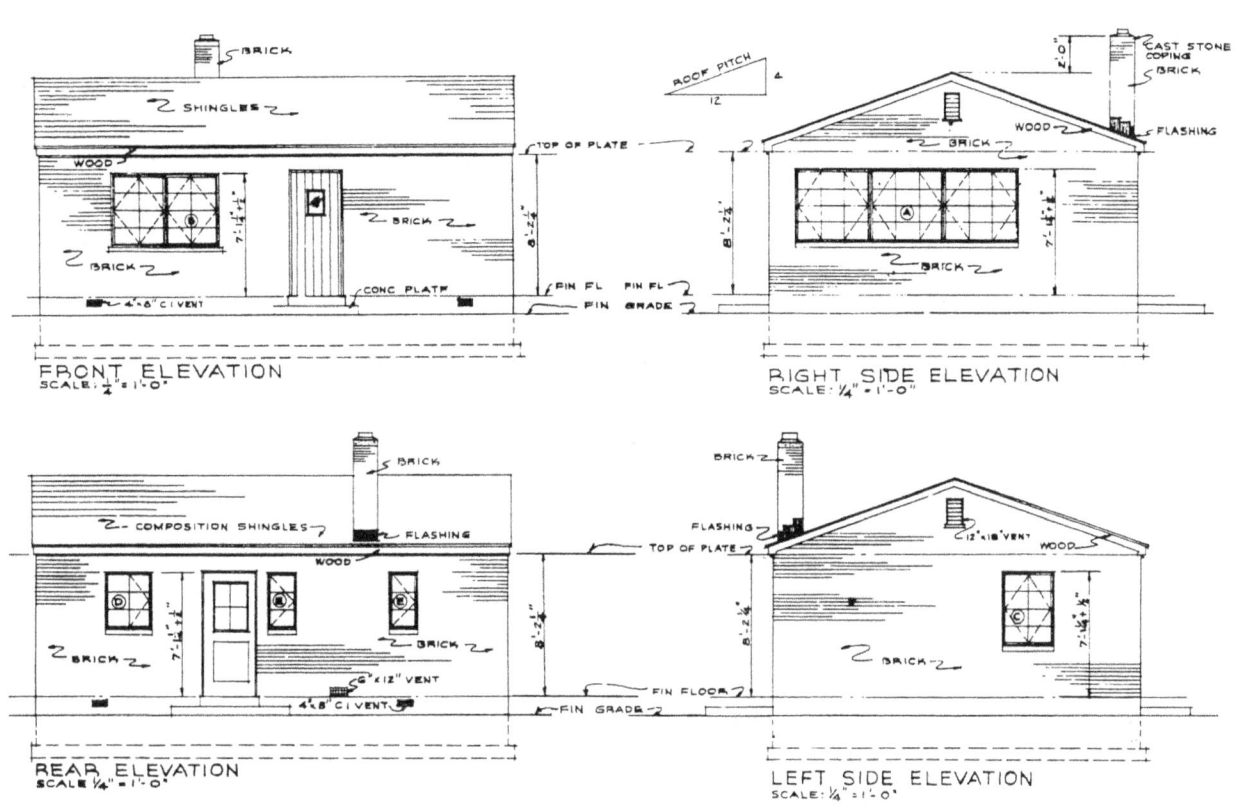

Figure 2-9.—Elevations.

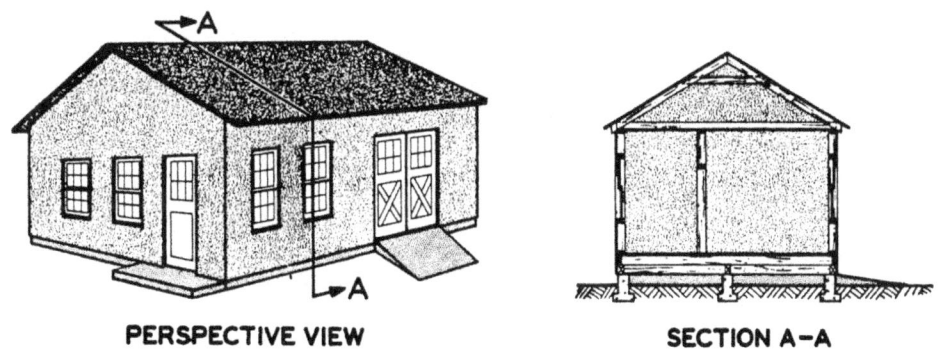

Figure 10.—Development of a section view.

All finishing hardware shall be installed in accordance with the manufacturers' directions. Calking and flashing shall be provided where indicated, or where necessary to provide weathertight construction.

Next after the General Requirements for Carpentry and Joinery, there is generally a subsection on "Grading," in which the kinds and grades of the various woods to be used in the structure are specified. Subsequent subsections

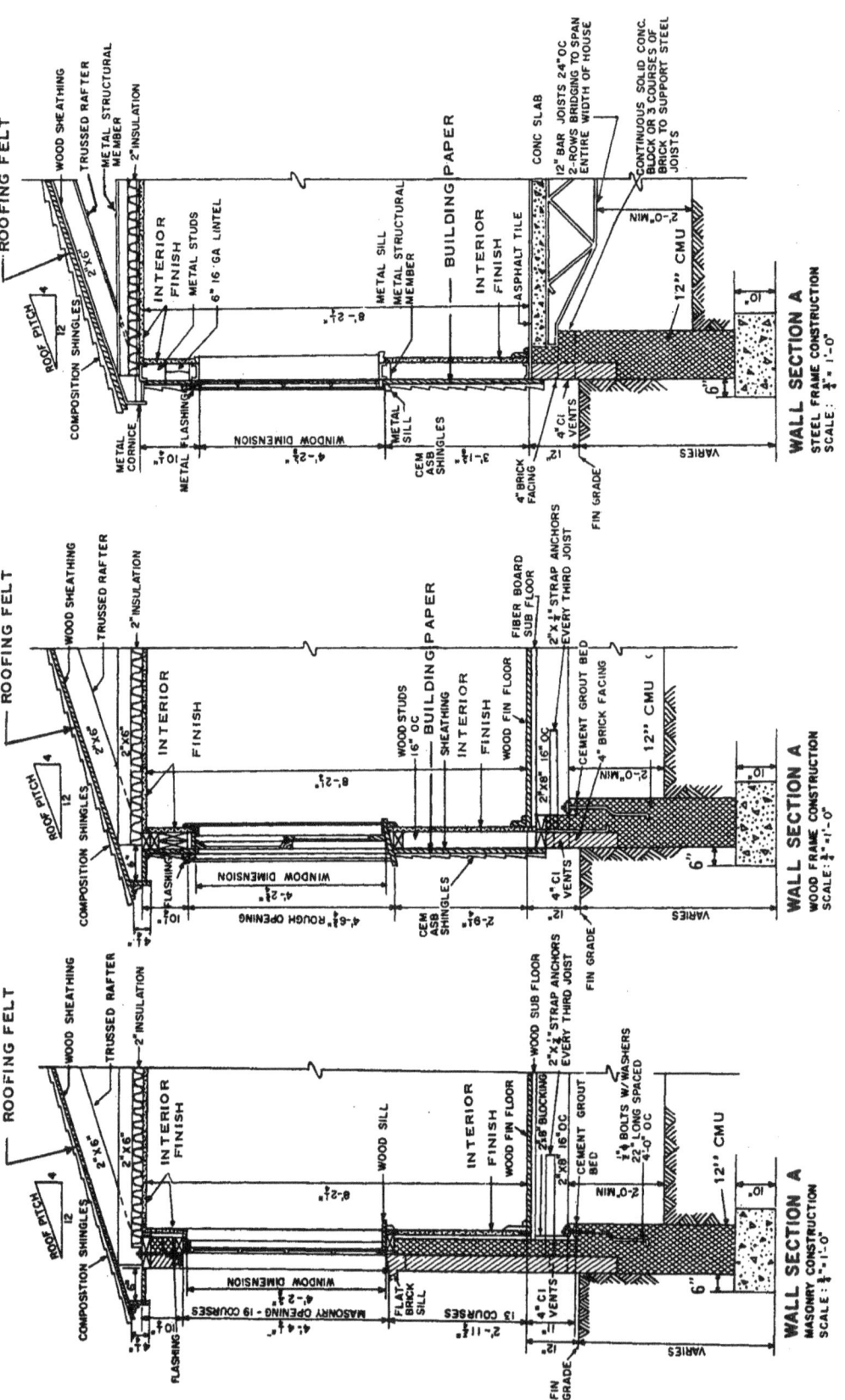

Figure 11.—Wall sections

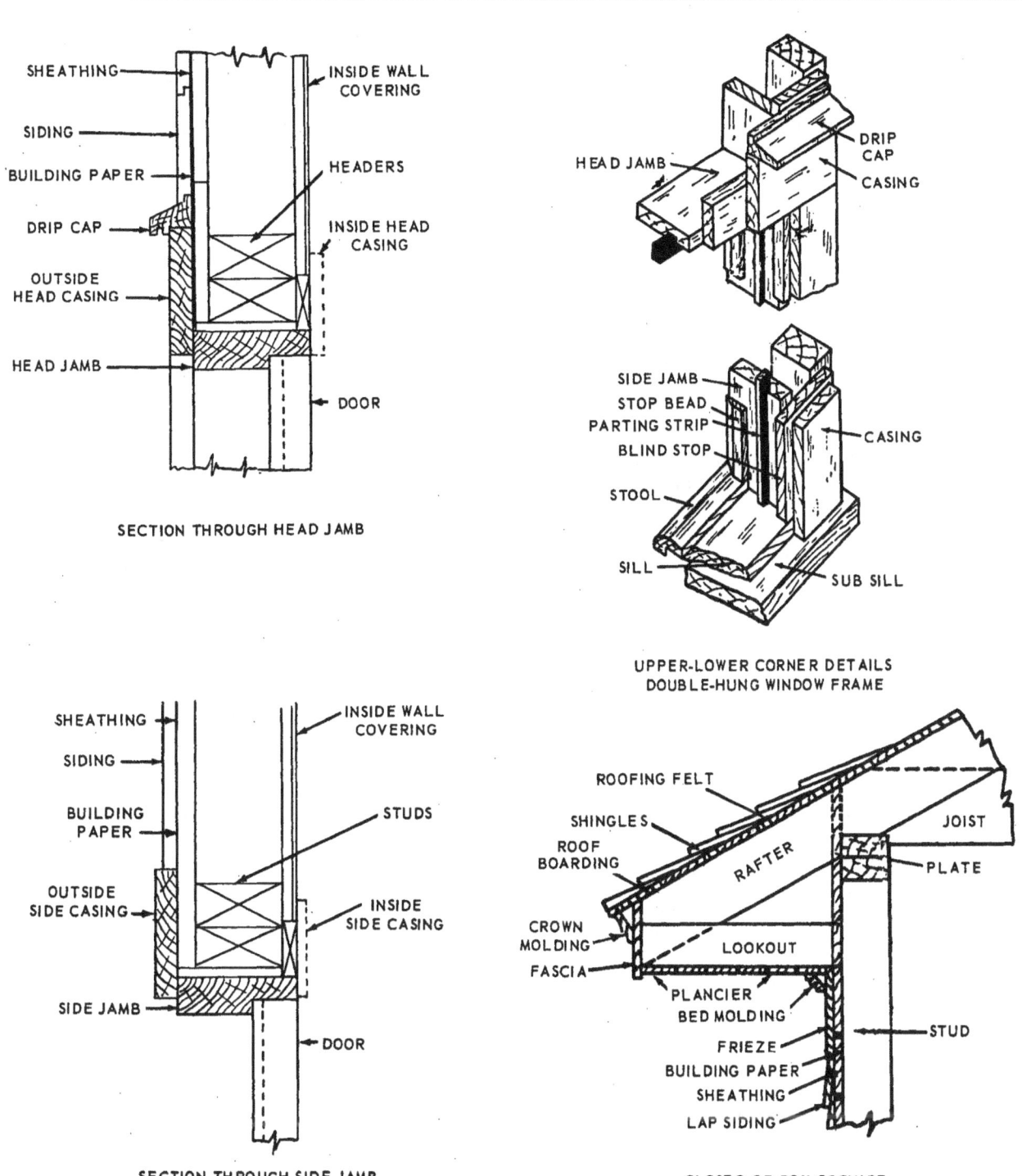

Figure 12.—Door, window and eave details.

specify various quality criteria and standards of workmanship for the various aspects of the rough and finish carpentry work, under such headings as FRAMING; SILLS, PLATES, AND GIRDERS; FLOOR JOISTS AND ROOF RAFTERS; STUDDING; and so on. An example of one of these subsections follows:

STUDDING for walls and partitions shall have doubled plates and doubled stud caps. Studs shall be set plumb and not to exceed 16-in. centers and in true alignment; they shall be bridged with one row of 2 x 4 pieces, set flatwise, fitted tightly, and nailed securely to each stud. Studding shall be doubled around openings and the heads of openings shall rest on the inner studs. Openings in partitions having widths of 4 ft and over shall be trussed. In wood frame construction, studs shall be trebled at corners to form posts.

From the above samples, you can see that a knowledge of the relevant specifications is as essential to the construction supervisor and the construction artisan as a knowledge of the construction drawings.

It is very important that the proper spec be used to cover the material requested. In cases in which the material is not covered by a Government spec, the ASTM (American Society for Testing Materials) spec or some other approved commercial spec may be used. It is EXTREMELY IMPORTANT in using specifications to cite all amendments, including the latest changes.

As a rule, the specs are provided for each project by the A/E (ARCHITECT-ENGINEERS). These are the OFFICIAL guidelines approved by the chief engineer or his representative for use during construction. These requirements should NOT be deviated from without prior approval from proper authority. This approval is usually obtained by means of a change order. When there is disagreement between the specifications and drawings, the specifications should normally be followed; however, check with higher authority in each case.

IV. BUILDER'S MATHEMATICS

The Builder has many occasions for the employment of the processes of ordinary arithmetic, and he must be thoroughly familiar with the methods of determining the areas and volumes of the various plane and solid geometrical figures. Only a few practical applications and a few practical suggestions, will be given here.

RATIO AND PROPORTION

There are a great many practical applications of ratio and proportion in the construction field. A few examples are as follows:

Some dimensions on construction drawings (such as, for example, distances from base lines and elevations of surfaces) are given in ENGINEER'S instead of CARPENTER's measure. Engineer's measure is measure in feet and decimal parts of a foot, or in inches and decimal parts of an inch, such as 100.15 ft or 11.14 in. Carpenter's measure is measure in yards, feet, inches, and even-denominator fractions of an inch, such as 1/2 in., 1/4 in., 1/16 in., 1/32 in., and 1/64 in.

You must know how to convert an engineer's measure given on a construction drawing to a carpenter's measure. Besides this, it will often happen that calculations you make yourself may produce a result in feet and decimal parts of a foot, which result you will have to convert to carpenter's measure. To convert engineer's to carpenter's measure you can use ratio and proportion as follows:

Let's say that you want to convert 100.14 ft to feet and inches to the nearest 1/16 in. The 100 you don't need to convert, since it is already in feet. What you need to do, first, is to find out how many twelfths of a foot (that is, how many inches) there are in 14/100 ft. Set this up as a proportional equation as follows: x:12::14:100.

You know that in a proportional equation the product of the means equals the product of the extremes. Consequently, $100x = (12 \times 14)$, or 168. Then $x = 168/100$, or 1.68 in. Next question is, how many 16ths of an in. are there in 68/100 in.? Set this up, too, as a proportional equation, thus: x:16::68:100. Then $100x = 1088$, and $x = 10\ 88/100$ sixteenths. Since 88/100 of a sixteenth is more than one-half of a sixteenth, you ROUND OFF by calling it 11/16. In 100.14 ft, then, there are 100 ft 1 11/16 in. For example:

A. means
$$\underbrace{x:12::14:100}_{\text{Extremes}}$$

Product of extremes = product of means:

$$100\,x = 168$$
$$x = 1.68 \text{ IN.}$$

B. x:16::68:100

$$100\,x = 1088$$

$$x = 10.88$$

$$x = 10\,\frac{88}{100}\text{ sixteenths}$$

Rounded off to 11/16

Another way to convert engineer's measurements to carpenter's measurements is to multiply the decimal portion of a foot by 12 to get inches; multiply the decimal by 16 to get the fraction of an inch.

There are many other practical applications of ratio and proportion in the construction field. Suppose, for example, that a table tells you that, for the size and type of brick wall you happen to be laying, 12,321 bricks and 195 cu ft of mortar are required per every 1000 sq ft of wall. How many bricks and how much mortar will be needed for 750 sq ft of the same wall? You simply set up equations as follows; for example:

Brick: x:750::12,321:1000
Mortar: x:750::195:1000

Brick: $\frac{X}{750} = \frac{12,321}{1000}$ Cross multiply

$$1000\,X = 9,240,750 \quad \text{Divide}$$
$$X = 9,240.75 = 9241 \text{ Brick.}$$

Mortar: $\frac{X}{750} = \frac{195}{1000}$ Cross multiply

$$1000\,X = 146,250 \quad \text{Divide}$$
$$X = 146.25 = 146\,1/4 \text{ cu ft}$$

Suppose, for another example, that the ingredient proportions by volume for the type of concrete you are making are 1 cu ft cement to 1.7 cu ft sand to 2.8 cu ft coarse aggregate. Suppose you know as well, by reference to a table, that ingredients combined in the amounts indicated will produce 4.07 cu ft of concrete. How much of each ingredient will be required to make a cu yd of concrete?

Remember here, first, that there are not 9, but 27 (3 ft x 3 ft x 3 ft) cu ft in a cu yd. Your proportional equations will be as follows:

Cement: x:27::1:4.07

Sand: x:27::1.7:4.07

Coarse aggregate: x:27::2.8:4.07

Cement: x:27::1:4.07

$$\frac{x}{27} = \frac{1}{4.07}$$

$$4.07\,x = 27$$

$$x = 6.63 \text{ cu ft Cement}$$

Sand: x:27::1.7:4.07

$$\frac{x}{27} = \frac{1.7}{4.07}$$

$$4.07\,x = 45.9$$

$$x = 11.28 \text{ cu ft Sand}$$

Coarse aggregate: x:27::2.8:407

$$\frac{x}{27} = \frac{2.8}{4.07}$$

$$4.07\,x = 75.6$$

$$x = 18.57 \text{ cu ft Coarse aggregate}$$

ARITHMETICAL OPERATIONS

The formulas for finding the area and volume of geometric figures are expressed in algebraic equations which are called formulas. A few of the more important formulas and their mathematical solutions will be discussed in this section.

To get an area, you multiply 2 linear measures together, and to get a volume you multiply 3 linear measures together. The linear measures you multiply together must all be expressed in the SAME UNITS; you cannot, for example, multiply a length in feet by a width in inches to get a result in square feet or in square inches.

Dimensions of a feature on a construction drawing are not always given in the same units. For a concrete wall, for example, the length and height are usually given in feet and the thickness in inches. Furthermore, you may want to get a result in units which are different from any shown on the drawing. Concrete volume, for example, is usually expressed in cubic yards, while the dimensions of concrete work are given on the drawings in feet and inches.

You can save yourself a good many steps in calculating by using fractions to convert the original dimension units into the desired end-result units. Take 1 in., for example. To express 1 in. in feet, you simply put it over 12, thus: 1/12 ft. To express 1 in. in yards, you simply put it over 36, thus: 1/36 yd. In the same manner, to express 1 ft in yards you simply put it over 3, thus 1/3 yd.

Suppose now that you want to calculate the number of cu yd of concrete in a wall 32 ft long by 14 ft high by 8 in. thick. You can express all these in yards and set up your problem thus:

$$\frac{32}{3} \times \frac{14}{3} \times \frac{8}{36}$$

Next you can cancel out, thus:

$$\frac{\overset{16}{\cancel{32}}}{3} \times \frac{\cancel{14}}{3} \times \frac{8}{\underset{9}{\cancel{\underset{18}{\cancel{36}}}}} = \frac{896}{81}$$

Dividing 896 by 81, you get 11.06 cu yds of concrete in the wall.

The right triangle is a triangle which contains one right (90°) angle. The following letters will denote the parts of the triangle indicated in figure 2-13—a = altitude, b = base, c = hypotenuse.

In solving a right triangle, the length of any side may be found if the lengths of the other two sides are given. The combinations of 3-4-5 (lengths of sides) or any multiple of these combinations will come out to a whole number. The following examples show the formula for finding

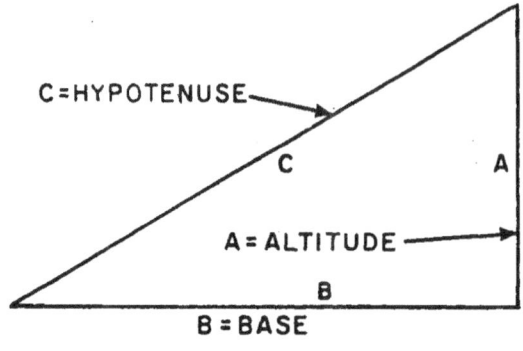

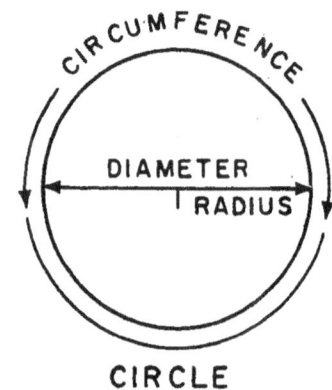

Figure 13.—Right triangle and circle.

each side. Each of these formulas is derived from the master formula $c^2 = a^2 + b^2$.

(1) Find c when a = 3, and b = 4.

$$c = \sqrt{a^2 + b^2} = \sqrt{3^2 + 4^2} = \sqrt{9 + 16} = \sqrt{25} = 5$$

(2) Find a when b = 8, and c = 10.

$$a = \sqrt{c^2 - b^2} = \sqrt{10^2 - 8^2} = \sqrt{100 - 64} = \sqrt{36} = 6$$

(3) Find b when a = 9, and c = 15.

$$b = \sqrt{c^2 - a^2} = \sqrt{15^2 - 9^2} = \sqrt{225 - 81} = \sqrt{144} = 12.$$

There are tables from which the square roots of numbers may be found; otherwise, they may be found arithmetically as explained later in this chapter.

Areas And Volumes Of
Geometric Figures

This section on areas and volumes of geometric figures will be limited to the most commonly used geometric figures. Reference books, such as Mathematics, Vol. 1, are available for additional information if needed. Areas are expressed in square units and volumes in cubic units.

1. A circle is a plane figure bounded by a curved line every point of which is the same distance from the center.
    a. The curved line is called the circumference.
    b. A straight line drawn from the center to any point on the circumference is called a radius. (r = 1/2 the diameter.)
    c. A straight line drawn from one point of the circumference through the center and terminating on the opposite point of the circumference is called a diameter. (d = 2 times the radius.) See figure 2-13.
    d. The area of a circle is found by the following formulas: $A = \pi r^2$ or $A = .7854 d^2$. (π is pronounced pie = 3.1416 or 3 1/7, .7854 is 1/4 of π.) Example: Find the area of a circle whose radius is 7". $A = \pi r^2 = 3\ 1/7 \times 7^2 = 22/7 \times 49 = 154$ sq in. If you use the second formula you obtain the same results.
    e. The circumference of a circle is found by multiplying π times the diameter or 2 times π times the radius. Example: Find the circumference of a circle whose diameter is 56 inches. $C = \pi d = 3.1415 \times 56 = 175.9296$ inches.

2. The area of a right triangle is equal to one-half the product of the base by the altitude. (Area = 1/2 base x altitude.) Example: Find the area of a triangle whose base is 16" and altitude 6". Solution:

$$A = 1/2\ bh = 1/2 \times 16 \times 6 = 48 \text{ sq in.}$$

3. The volume of a cylinder is found by multiplying the area of the base times the height. ($V = 3.1416 \times r^2 \times h$). Example: Find the volume of a cylinder which has a radius of 8 in. and a height of 4 ft. Solution:

$$8 \text{ in} = \frac{2}{3} \text{ ft and } \left(\frac{2}{3}\right)2 = \frac{4}{9} \text{ sq ft.}$$

$$V = 3.1416 \times \frac{4}{9} \times 4 = \frac{50.2656}{9} = 5.59 \text{ cu ft.}$$

4. The volume of a rectangular solid equals the length x width x height. (V = lwh.) Example: Find the volume of a rectangular solid which has a length of 6 ft, a width of 3 ft, and a height of 2 ft. Solution:

$$V = lwh = 6 \times 3 \times 2 = 36 \text{ cu ft.}$$

5. The volume of a cone may be found by multiplying one-third times the area of the base times the height.

$$\left(V = \frac{1}{3} \pi r^2 h\right)$$

Example: Find the volume of a cone when the radius of its base is 2 ft and its height is 9 ft. Solution:

$$\pi = 3.1416,\ r = 2,\ 2^2 = 4$$

$$V = \frac{1}{3} r^2 h = \frac{1}{3} \times 3.1416 \times 4 \times 9 = 37.70 \text{ cu ft.}$$

Powers And Roots

1. Powers—When we multiply several numbers together, as 2 x 3 x 4 = 24, the numbers 2, 3, and 4 are factors and 24 the product. The operation of raising a number to a power is a special case of multiplication in which the factors are all equal. The power of a number is the number of times the number itself is to be taken as a factor. Example: 2^4 is 16. The second power is called the square of the number, as 3^2. The third power of a number is called the cube of the number, as 5^3. The exponent of a number is a number placed to the right and above a base to show how many times the base is used as a factor. Example:

$$4^3 \xleftarrow{} \text{exponent} = \text{base}$$

$$4 \times 4 \times 4 = 64.$$

2. Roots—To indicate a root, use the sign $\sqrt{}$, which is called the radical sign. A small figure, called the index of the root, is placed in the opening of the sign to show which root is to be taken. The square root of a number is one of the two equal factors into which a number is

divided. Example: $\sqrt{81} = \sqrt{9 \times 9} = 9$. The cube root is one of the three equal factors into which a number is divided. Example: $\sqrt[3]{125} = \sqrt[3]{5 \times 5 \times 5} = 5$.

Square Root

1. The square root of any number is that number which, when multiplied by itself, will produce the first number. For example; the square root of 121 is 11 because 11 times 11 equals 121.

2. How to extract the square root arithmetically:

$$\sqrt{9025} \quad \sqrt{90'25.}^{\,95.}$$

```
          : -81

    180 : 925
    +5  : -925

    185 : 000
```

a. Begin at the decimal point and divide the given number into groups of 2 digits each (as far as possible), going from right to left and/or left to right.
b. Find the greatest number (9) whose square is contained in the first or left hand group (90). Square this number (9) and place it under the first pair of digits (90), then subtract.
c. Bring down the next pair of digits (25) and add it to the remainder (9).
d. Multiply the first digit in the root by 20 and use it as a trial divisor (180). This trial divisor (180) will go into the new dividend (925) five times. This number, 5 (second digit in the root), is added back to the trial divisor, obtaining the true divisor (185).
e. The true divisor (185) is multiplied by the second digit (5) and placed under the remainder (925). Subtract and the problem is solved.
f. If there is still a remainder and you want to carry the problem further, add zeros (in pairs) and continue the above process.

Coverage Calculations

You will frequently have occasion to estimate the number of linear feet of boards of a given size, or the number of tiles, asbestos shingles, and the like, required to cover a given area. Let's take the matter of linear feet of boards first.

What you do here is calculate, first, the number of linear feet of board required to cover 1 sq ft. For boards laid edge-to-edge, you base your calculations on the total width of a board. For boards which will lap each other, you base your calculations on the width laid TO THE WEATHER, meaning the total width minus the width of the lap.

Since there are 144 sq in. in a sq ft, linear footage to cover a given area can be calculated as follows. Suppose your boards are to be laid 8 in. to the weather. If you divide 8 in. into 144 sq in., the result (which is 18 in., or 1.5 ft) will be the linear footage required to cover a sq ft. If you have, say, 100 sq ft to cover, the linear footage required will be 100 x 1.5, or 150 ft.

To estimate the number of tiles, asbestos shingles, and the like required to cover a given area, you first calculate the number of units required to cover a sq ft. Suppose, for example, you are dealing with 9 in. x 9 in. asphalt tiles. The area of one of these is 9 in. x 9 in. or 81 sq in. In a sq ft there are 144 sq in. If it takes 1 to cover 81 sq in., how many will it take to cover 144 sq in.? Just set up a proportional equation, as follows.

$$1:81::x:144$$

When you work this out, you will find that it takes 1.77 tiles to cover a sq ft. To find the number of tiles required to cover 100 sq ft, simply multiply by 100. How do you multiply anything by 100? Just move the decimal point 2 places to the right. Consequently, it takes 177 9 x 9 asphalt tiles to cover 100 sq ft of area.

Board Measure

BOARD MEASURE is a method of measuring lumber in which the basic unit is an abstract volume 1 ft long by 1 ft wide by 1 in. thick. This abstract volume or unit is called a BOARD FOOT.

There are several formulas for calculating the number of board feet in a piece of given dimensions. Since lumber dimensions are most frequently indicated by width and thickness in inches and length in feet, the following formula is probably the most practical.

$$\frac{\text{Thickness in in.} \times \text{width in in.} \times \text{length in ft}}{12}$$

= board feet

Suppose you are calculating the number of board feet in a 14-ft length of 2 x 4. Applying the formula, you get:

$$\frac{\overset{1}{\cancel{2}} \times \overset{2}{\cancel{4}} \times 14}{\underset{\underset{3}{\cancel{\cancel{6}}}}{\cancel{12}}} = \frac{28}{3} = 9\ 1/3 \text{ bd ft}$$

The chief practical use of board measure is in cost calculations, since lumber is bought and sold by the board foot. Any lumber less than 1 in. thick is presumed to be 1 in. thick for board measure purposes. Board measure is calculated on the basis of the NOMINAL, not the ACTUAL, dimensions of lumber.

The actual size of a piece of dimension lumber (such as a 2 x 4, for example) is usually less than the nominal size.